# NVQs, Standards and Competence

# NVQs, Standards and Competence

## A Practical Guide for Employers, Managers and Trainers

**Shirley Fletcher**

KOGAN PAGE

Published in association with
Godfrey Durham Training
Consultants Ltd

## To Dale and Kelly

First published in 1991

Apart from any fair dealing for the purposes of research or private study, or criticism or review, as permitted under the Copyright, Designs and Patents Act, 1988, this publication may only be reproduced, stored or transmitted, in any form or by any means, with the prior permission in writing of the publishers, or in the case of reprographic reproduction in accordance with the terms of licences issued by the Copyright Licensing Agency. Enquiries concerning reproduction outside those terms should be sent to the publishers at the undermentioned address:

Kogan Page Limited
120 Pentonville Road
London N1 9JN

© Shirley Fletcher, 1991

**British Library Cataloguing in Publication Data**
A CIP record for this book is available from the British Library.

ISBN 0 7494 0365 9

Typeset by AsTec, Newport, Saffron Walden, Essex

Printed and bound in Great Britain by Biddles Ltd, Guildford

# Contents

CONTENTS

# Acknowledgements

The author wishes to acknowledge contributions from the following individuals and organisations. Some of them she has worked with closely in the past; others, not currently clients, kindly responded to a request for information.

All the individuals concerned supplied helpful information and gave generously of their time despite a tight schedule. The author would like to record her appreciation for their involvement.

| | |
|---|---|
| John Wigglesworth<br>  Training Manager | Post Office Counters Ltd |
| Jackie Hall<br>  APL Project Director | Management Charter Institute |
| Gerry Rose<br>  Training Manager,<br>  Operations | United Distillers |
| Peter Aley<br>  Director, Strategic Plans<br>  and Co-ordination | Association of British Travel Agents National Training Board |
| Sue Stephens | Association of British Travel National Training Board<br>British Steel |
| Colin Green<br>  Manager,<br>  Central Training Unit | |
| Lyn Martin<br>  Assistant Principal<br>  (Curriculum) | Coventry Technical College |

| Chris Brown | Scotvec |
| Barras Stone | British Gas |
|    Training Development | |
|    Manager | |
| John Bailey | British Gas |
|    Manager, Functional | |
|    Training | |
| Gail Stirling | Institute of |
|    Director, Professional | Chartered Secretaries and |
|    Development & Educa- | Administrators |
|    tion | |

# Preface

As new competence-based standards and National Vocational Qualifications are tested and introduced across all industries, the need for practical help becomes more acute. This book aims to provide such help.

For most companies, a detailed understanding of the technicalities of standards development will not be required. However, a brief review of technical details is provided to assist understanding of the key concepts and issues which underlie the new structure of standards and assessment. Readers interested in further technical information will find the reference section of assistance. Those who require guidance on specific questions should turn to the 'Quick Reference Guide' in the Help Menu (p 183).

Part I provides employers and managers with a strategic overview of recent developments in the field of competence-based provision, with specific emphasis on the potential benefits and challenges that these developments present for companies in the UK. Key questions and checklists to aid decision-making are included. Part I will also be of interest to senior training staff and to personnel professionals who need to know more about the purpose, structure and resource implications of implementing recent actions for change.

Part II takes training practitioners, and those with responsibility for 'hands on' implementation of change, step by step through the introduction of NVQs and the various uses of competence-based standards. The final chapters provide a brief overview and general guidance on how to make the best use of new competence-based developments within your company.

Checklists and charts provide user-friendly reference documents.

Case studies, provided by companies who are (or will shortly be) implementing standards and/or NVQs, bring to life the practical application of these new structures and processes. Features from the Management Charter Initiative, from an Industry Lead Body, from a college, and from a professional body are also included to give the reader an overall perspective of developments.

The Help Menu in Part III is the practitioner's reference file on who to contact and how to get information on a range of topics. References for further reading and technical information are also included.

# PART 1
# The Company Perspective: Understanding and Planning

# Introduction

- What are NVQs?
- What are standards of occupational competence?
- Why should my company introduce them?
- What are the resource implications?
- How do we get these standards?
- What do we do with them when we have them?
- Why do we have to change from the old system of standards and qualifications?

These are just some of the questions currently being asked by employers, managers and trainers across all industries in the UK. Many more such questions are listed in The Quick Reference Guide on page 183, along with the sections where readers will find the answers. But for many people, perhaps the biggest question is why these changes are taking place at all.

## Backdrop to developments

During the 1980s a clear picture emerged in the UK – reports outlined imminent demographic changes, an unstable employment market, a 'skills gap' and a lack of economic competition with our European neighbours. It became apparent that the UK vocational education and training (VET) system was unable to meet the demand for the skilled workforce that employers needed.

In 1981, the then Manpower Services Commission (MSC)

produced its *New Training Initiative: An Agenda for Action* (MSC 1981). The key theme of this document was the clearly identified need for Britain to develop a 'flexible, adaptable workforce to cope with the uncertainties that cloud the future'. It suggested that there were two crucial components to this development:

- a comprehensive training strategy
- standards of a new kind.

The new strategy became the three NTI objectives:

- develop skills training
- equip all young people for work
- widen opportunities for adults.

One of the most important aspects of this overall strategy how-ever, lies in one simple phrase: 'at the heart of the initiative lie standards of a new kind' (MSC 1981).

The new strategy depended upon these new standards becoming available. However, initially, there was confusion about the concept. Didn't we already have standards? What about British Standards? Did the document mean 'training standards' or 'standards required in the workplace'?

## Competence, standards and qualifications

Before long, the idea of a 'new kind of standard' became linked to the term 'competence'. The idea of a 'flexible and adaptable workforce' was superseded by that of a 'competent' one as reports such as *A Challenge to Complacency* (Coopers and Lybrand 1985) and *Competence and Competition* created an impact in the training world.

In 1986, the government published a White Paper, *Working Together, Education and Training* (HMSO 1986) which set out plans for a radical review of the UK education and training system. As the title of the paper suggests, a key focus was greater partnership between the providers and users of both education and training. One of the paper's key objectives was to ensure that 'competence and achievement are recognised and rewarded'. It stated that 'arrangements for standard setting and assessment also need improvement' and proposed that 'the structure of vocational qualificatons be reformed'.

A report produced earlier that year, *Review of Vocational Qualifications in England and Wales* (MSC/NEDC 1986), had suggested that the existing system of vocational qualifications lacked a clear, readily understandable pattern of provision while suffering from considerable overlap and gaps in provision. It also suggested that there were many barriers to access to qualifications and inadequate arrangements for progression and/or transfer of credit. Finally, it suggested that assessment methods tended to be biased towards testing of knowledge rather than skill or competence, when what was needed by employers was application of skills and knowledge.

The report suggested that a vocational qualification should be defined as:

a statement of competence, clearly relevant to work and intended to facilitate entry into, or progression in employment, further education and training, issued by a recognised body to an individual.

It also suggested that this statement of competence should incorporate assessment of:

- skills to specified standards
- relevant knowledge and understanding
- the ability to use skills and to apply knowledge
- and understanding to the performance of relevant tasks.

The government White Paper took all these recommendations forward and solidly agreed that 'vocational qualifications need to relate more directly and clearly to competence required (and acquired) in work'. The radical reform of vocational qualifications therefore became a priority development area.

## What are the benefits?

The basic assumptions on which the new system of standards and qualifications operates are that training and work performance can be improved if people know exactly what is expected of them *within the working role*, and if they can be assessed reliably against those standards. In addition, if the expectations are defined by industry itself as explicit standards, and are agreed across industry, then recruitment, selection and maintenance of high standards across the UK can also be improved.

As many companies have found, the key benefits of the new system include increased flexibility of training, an improvement in the identification of training needs and involvement of all staff at all levels in the overall performance (and therefore profitability) of the company.

This is not to say, of course, that the new system is a cure-all for economic problems at either macro or micro level; nor is it a five-minute wonder in terms of the investment required to implement it.

If your company is considering introducing competence-based standards and NVQs, this introduction must be planned, and staff must be trained in its operation. The case studies provided by companies who have begun this work illustrate the importance of these two aspects of change.

## Myths and misconceptions

Two main myths/misconceptions hamper understanding of the new structure of standards and qualifications.

### NVQs are not training programmes

Many people perceive the new form of qualifications (NVQs,

and SVQs in Scotland) as specified training programmes. The 'unit-based structure' of NVQs/SVQs becomes confused with 'modular training programmes'. The point will be clearly made throughout this book that NVQs are not training programmes. A unit of competence is a unit of *Assessment* – it contains explicit standards of workplace performance. Readers should refer to Chapters 2, 3, 4 and 12 for further clarification.

## NVQs are not awarded by the NCVQ

A second misconception is that the National Council for Vocational Qualifications (NCVQ) is the awarding body for this new form of certificate. NCVQ is *not* an awarding body, it is an *accrediting body*. NVQs will be awarded by traditional bodies, such as City and Guilds, RSA, BTEC in England and Wales; SVQs will be awarded by Scotvec in Scotland. In addition, some Industry Lead Bodies have become joint awarding bodies. NCVQ puts its stamp of approval on those qualifications which meet its criteria. Readers should refer to Chapters 2, 3, 4 and 11 for further information.

Of course other misunderstandings also occur. These are dealt with in the relevant sections of this book. The reader will find the Quick Reference Guide (p 183) of help in locating answers to particular questions.

# Chapter 1

# *Actions for Change*

## 1.1 New standards

Following publication of the government White Paper *Working Together, Education and Training* (HMSO 1986), action to introduce a new kind of standard and new forms of vocational qualifications were taken. The government directed the Manpower Services Commission (MSC, now the Training Agency) to:

> put in place dependable arrangements for setting standards of occupational competence across all sectors of industry

It was agreed that these new standards should be defined *by industry* – a dramatic change from traditional forms of standard-setting – and should address questions such as the following:

- Who are the gatekeepers of standards for occupational performance of your workforce?
- Where are these standards?
- Are they accessible to all staff?
- Are they explicit?
- Do they represent expectations of performance or do they reflect what people need to know?

You might consider what your own answers to these questions would be. Traditionally, standards were embedded in curricula: they represented the *inputs* of training – what people had to learn. Assessment has in the past been biased towards testing of knowledge. Here was a shift to standards, and to associated assessment systems, which were to specify and assess *outputs* – what people had to *achieve*.

It is employers who recruit and employ staff, and it is employers who have expectations of the performance of those staff. It follows that employers and industry representatives should set the standards.

## 1.2 The standards programme

In order to achieve this, the MSC contacted all remaining Industrial Training Boards (ITBs) and Non-Statutory Training Organisations (NSTOs) and, through a series of conferences organised by the 'Industry Lead Body' (see below) and new 'Occupational Standards Branches' of MSC's head office, put into action a programme of development.

ITBs and NSTOs, as the bodies with responsibility for training within all sectors of industry, were each asked to supply an action plan to provide the following detail:

- occupations for which each ITB/NSTO had training responsibility
- a timescale for the development of standards of occupational competence for each occupation
- a timescale for the development of new National Vocational Qualifications (NVQs) for each occupation
- an estimated cost of development.

This information enabled the MSC to prepare an 'occupational map' in an attempt to ensure that all occupations across all sectors of all industries would achieve the development of new standards and NVQs.

Where ITBs and NSTOs did not exist (for example in the care sector), a long process of negotiation with a wide range of sectoral organisations began. Representatives from all areas of sectoral activity were brought together and a new kind of organisation – the Industry Lead Body – was formed.

## 1.3   Industry Lead Bodies

Industry Lead Bodies are still being established across all sectors of industry and commerce. Their key responsibilities are the development of industry-defined standards of occupational competence and approval of a framework of new National Vocational Qualifications.

All new NVQs developed by industry need approval of the Industry Lead Body before they can be submitted to the National Council for Vocational Qualifications (NCVQ) for final approval.

Funding for the development of standards and NVQs was provided in part by government. The MSC contributed up to 50 per cent of development costs and provided project managers from The Occupational Standards Branch. The remaining 50 per cent of costs had to be provided by the industry, usually in the form of staff time, accommodation for meetings and workshops, overheads, and so on.

## 1.4   The National Council for Vocational Qualifications (NCVQ)

Established in 1986, it was to be responsible for

> bringing vocational qualifications in England and Wales into a new national framework to be called the National Vocational Qualification (NVQ). (MSC/NEDC 1981)

Initially the new framework was to consist of four levels, based on the following descriptions of standards of achievement:

*Level 1*
Occupational competence in performing a range of tasks under supervision.
*Level 2*
Occupational competence in performing a wider, more demanding range of tasks with limited supervision.
*Level 3*
Occupational competence required for satisfactory responsible performance in a defined occupation or range of jobs.
*Level 4*
Competence to design and specify defined tasks, products and processes and to accept responsibility for the work of others.

Expansion to level 4+ was to be discussed and the first developments to be undertaken in this area began in 1989, following long discussion and negotiation with the 250 professional bodies.

## The role of the NCVQ

The government set nine specific tasks for the NCVQ:

- Identify and bring about the changes necessary to achieve the specification and implementation of standards of occupational competence to meet the needs of the full range of employment, including the needs of the self-employed
- Design, monitor and adapt as necessary the new NVQ framework
- Secure the implementation of that framework by accrediting the provision of approved certifying bodies
- Secure comprehensive provision of vocational qualifications by the certifying bodies
- Secure arrangements for quality assurance
- Maintain effective liaison with those bodies having responsibilities for qualifications which give entry to, and

progression within and from, the system of vocational qualifications into higher education and the higher levels of professional qualifications

- Collect, analyse and make available information on vocational qualifications and secure the operation of an effective, comprehensive and dependable database
- Undertake or arrange to be undertaken research and development where necessary to discharge these functions
- Promote the interests of vocational education and training, and, in particular, of vocational qualifications and disseminate good practice.

## The NCVQ and existing examining and validating bodies

The NCVQ has a new and unique role. It is not an *examining* body – it does not set standards or assess examination papers centrally. Neither is it a *validating* body – it does not approve centres to operate training or learning programmes which lead to the award of a qualification.

In order to understand the NCVQ's role, it is essential to grasp one key point:

**NVQS *have nothing whatsoever to do with training or learning programmes.***

The key is *assessment of performance*. How people learn, what training programme they undertake or what method of training or learning is employed is, in effect, irrelevant. To achieve an NVQ, an individual must *demonstrate competent performance*.

The NCVQ's role, therefore, is not the same as an existing examining or validating body. Its remit is to develop policy for the vocational qualifications system as a whole, to negotiate to achieve the stated objectives from the system and to accredit qualifications of bodies offering awards within the national qualification framework. The NCVQ, therefore, is an endorsing or accrediting body. It approves qualifications which meet its criteria. These criteria are explained fully in the following chapters.

## Scotland

The sole awarding body in Scotland is Scotvec, and they have been involved in all developments in England and Wales. The NCVQ's remit does not extend to Scotland, but new Scottish Vocational Qualifications (SVQs) will operate in conjunction with Industry Lead Bodies in the same way as those south of the border.

Scotland already has an operational credit accumulation plan (see Chapter 2) which was developed as a result of the 16+ Action Plan in the early 1980s. This credit accumulation system operates across the vocational education and training field and, like England and Wales, is being extended into the higher education and professional body arenas.

## 1.5  Implications for employers

The forces and actions for change which have briefly been explored in this chapter present new challenges and benefits for employers. Firstly, employers have been provided with an opportunity to directly influence the establishment of agreed standards of performance across all industries. Through representation on, and consultation with, Industry Lead Bodies, employers have been able to state exactly what they expect their workforce to do in each occupational role.

Second, this direct involvement in standard-setting has required employer investment – the standard setting-process takes considerable time and requires commitment to the overall concepts and objectives of the standards programme.

Third, a focus on performance in the workplace requires new forms of assessment of performance. Performance can be assessed most effectively *in the workplace*. Employers therefore have to consider how such workplace assessment systems will operate.

A fourth issue is that development and implementation of new standards and qualifications require a change in attitude.

Employers and their staff become much more involved in the individual development process. Assessment of performance in the workplace provides a solid foundation for training-needs analysis and more effective targeting of training. In the last decade, many reports have demonstrated that Britain is nowhere near the top of the list when it comes to investing in training and development of staff.

If employers are to reap the benefits of new standards which specify performance, which require workplace assessment, and which lead to national recognition of competent performance, should they not also be investing more in well-targeted training and development?

Last but by no means least is the issue of cost. These changes require an investment in development and a further investment in implementation. A key issue to be considered by users of the new systems of competence-based standards and qualifications is one of return on investment. What are the benefits of these new standards and qualifications?

A national, industry-wide perspective on current developments in competence-based standards and NVQs is provided in the following case study from the Association of British Travel Agents (ABTA) National Training Board, as Industry Lead Body for the travel agent and tour operator sector.

Case study

# THE ASSOCIATION OF BRITISH TRAVEL AGENTS NATIONAL TRAINING BOARD

## Background

The Association of British Travel Agents National Training Board (ABTA NTB) was established in July 1982. Its aims included operation of its own scheme of education and training for travel agents and tour operators, so that this sector of the travel industry could be master in its own house. (At a cost to ABTA members estimated to be about half that likely to be imposed by a statutory board.)

There are 3300 ABTA members comprising approx 2600 travel

agents, 350 tour operators and 350 companies which operate in both spheres. Between them, these have approximately 8000 outlets; members include a number of large chains such as Thomas Cook.

The National Training Board (NTB) has developed its own training facilities for use by the industry, including a college of open learning and computer-based training. It provides training services for the 100,000 employees in the sector. Its headquarters are in Woking, but some 40 per cent of NTB staff are regionally based and regularly visit members. The training board reports to the national council of ABTA but is otherwise autonomous and financially self-supporting.

Since 1982, ABTA NTB has grown. Its original staff complement of seven now exceeds 90, with over half its staff being training executives.

## ABTA and standards of competence

ABTA were early contributors to developments at national level regarding the introduction of NVQs. Standards for the industry had initially emerged through an industry-wide survey of companies selected to represent the spectrum of activities to be found in a travel agency. After circulation to ABTA member companies for detailed comment, the final outcome was the identification of competence levels required at the workplace for qualified counter clerks and qualified senior counter clerks as well as those for management roles.

## COTAC and COTAM

ABTA worked closely with City and Guilds to develop a qualification structure which became known as COTAC and COTAM – Certificate of Travel Agency Competence, and Certificate of Travel Agency Management.

Successful candidates on COTAC tests receive joint certification from City and Guilds and ABTA. A joint C&G/ABTA Travel Subject Certification Committee was established to maintain, monitor and further develop appropriate travel industry qualifications, consonant with the National Training Board holding sole responsibility for identifying and articulating competence standards and achievements.

In the ensuing ten years, a framework of qualifications has developed;

- The Certificate of Travel Agency Competence
  1. Qualified counter clerk – COTAC level 1
  2. Senior Counter clerk – COTAC level 2
- The Certificate of Travel Agency Management – COTAM

- The Certificate of Tour Operating Practice
  1. Qualified operative – COTOP level 1
  2. Senior clerk – COTOP level 2
- The Certificate in Travel skills – CITS

ABTA has certain delegated powers, as prescribed in a High Court Order in 1984. The Court established minimum staff qualifications for membership of ABTA (as a travel agency) as: (a) two years' relevant practical experience or (b) COTAC Level 1 (general) plus 18 months' practical experience or (c) COTAC level 2 (general) plus 12 months' relevant practical experience.

In 1986, ABTA NTB and City and Guilds introduced a progressive system of awards leading to the Licentiateship of City and Guilds for those working in retail travel. This scheme embraced the COTAC and COTAM tests and the legally prescribed period of relevant practical experience for ABTA membership purposes.

## ABTA and NCVQ

ABTA was among the first industry representative organisations to submit qualifications to the NCVQ for approval. The first, conditionally approved, NVQs were sanctioned by the NCVQ (shortly after its establishment), in mid-1987. The COTAC and COTAM qualification framework received conditional approval at NVQ levels 2 to 4. As this early approval was for a period of four years, and as 'conditions' have to be met for a further approval period to be granted, ABTA NTB is currently investing in the further development of qualifications for the industry to ensure that their award structure will meet state-of-the-art requirements.

Conditions attached to the original approval period included the removal of a time-serving period and the introduction of log-books for workplace records. ABTA has already made considerable progress in these areas. From June 1991, the NVQs at levels 2 and 3 will include work-based and assessed elements to replace the 18 months' and 12 months' work experience parts.

## Further developments

Since the original (conditional) approval of ABTA/City and Guilds awards in 1987, the criteria for approval of new NVQs have developed. The specification of standards in the form of elements, performance criteria and range statements has now been fully incorporated in

NCVQ guidance, as have explicit requirements regarding quality of associated assessment systems.

ABTA has remained up to date with these developments. Their new NVQ level 1 qualification has been prepared in the required format and will shortly be submitted to the NCVQ. They also plan to complete a full 'mapping exercise' of the industry to identify key work roles. Following final revision of the existing qualification structure, to reformat standards on a competence-base and develop work-based assessment structure, a complete NVQ framework will be put forward for final approval by the NCVQ. This framework will cover the three key ares of retail travel, tour operations and business travel.

## Assessor training and certification arrangements

ABTA is exploring the structure of assessor training and a work-based assessment model. For the initial pilot phase of the new NVQ level 1, staff of ABTA NTB will be trained and assessed against the City and Guilds 9293 award. These staff will then be able to deliver training to others.

The issue of verification of assessment is also being explored, with verifiers being appointed by the joint awarding body (ABTA NTB and City and Guilds). Once the assessment and verification models are clear, certification arrangements can be clarified.

ABTA NTB will continue to take the lead in the field of training and qualifications within the travel and tour operations sector. It has developed a three- to four-year plan in which all of these areas are addressed, and a qualification structure which meets national criteria and industry needs will be put in place.

# Chapter 2

# The New Structure

## 2.1 What is meant by competence?

New occupational standards are based on a concept of competence which emerged through long debate. The theoretical discussions regarding a precise definition are adequately covered in a wide range of technical papers. What is of key interest to employers is the applicability of the concept to the real-life employment arena.

The simplest definition of the new concept of competence is:

**the ability to perform activities within an occupation.**

However, this says nothing about how well the activities have to be performed! The gradual emergence of a more explicit definition occurred as attempts to define clear and meaningful standards continued:

> competence is a wide concept which embodies the ability to transfer skills and knowledge to new situations within the occupational area. It encompasses organisation and planning of work, innovation and coping with non-routine activities. It includes those qualities of personal effectiveness that are required in the workplace to deal with co-workers, managers and customers. (Training Agency 1988/89)

This broad, if lengthy, definition attempts to cover all aspects of 'competent' performance in a realistic working environment.

## 2.2 What exactly *are* NVQs?

The formal definition of a new National Vocational Qualification is that it is 'a statement of competence' which incorporates specified standards in 'the ability to perform in a range of work-related activities, the skills, knowledge and understanding which underpin such performance in employment' (Training Agency 1988/89).

Each NVQ covers a particular area of work, at a specific level of achievement and fits into the NVQ framework.

### The NVQ framework

The initial NVQ framework had four levels (level 4+ has been under discussion with the 250 UK professional bodies for some time).

| | Areas of work | | | |
|---|---|---|---|---|
| 1 | | | | |
| 2 | | | | |
| 3 | | | | |
| 4 | | | | |

**Figure 2.1** *NVQ framework*

The levels indicate competence achieved. Level descriptors are given in Figure 2.2.

'Areas of work' refer to occupations such as engineering, catering, agriculture and so on. Various reports on 'occupational mapping' have been carried out in recent years, the most widely known being TOC (training occupations classification). The NCVQ has reviewed the various classifications and also

*Level 1*
Competence in the performance of work activities which are in the main routine and predictable or provide a broad foundation, primarily as a basis for progression.

*Level 2*
Competence in a broader and more demanding range of work activities involving greater individual responsibility and autonomy than at level 1.

*Level 3*
Competence in skilled areas that involve performance of a broad range of work activities, including many that are complex and non-routine. In some areas, supervisory competence may be a requirement at this level.

*Level 4*
Competence in the performance of complex, technical, specialised and professional work activities, including those involving design, planning and problem-solving, with a significant degree of personal accountability. In many areas competence in supervision or management will be a requirement at this level.

**Figure 2.2** *NVQ framework – level descriptors*
*Source:* NCVQ 1988a

the information provided by Industry Lead Bodies as part of its 'mapping exercise' for standards development. This review has led to a new categorisation of occupations which now forms the basis of the NCVQ database of standards and qualifications.

## What do NVQs look like?

The unit-based structure of NVQs provides a hierarchical model of qualifications with standards forming the foundation stones.

As we have noted, the NVQ itself is a statement of competence which can be achieved through accumulation of 'credit' in the form of units of competence. Each unit is made up of defined standards of competence. The structure of an NVQ can therefore be illustrated as in Figure 2.3.

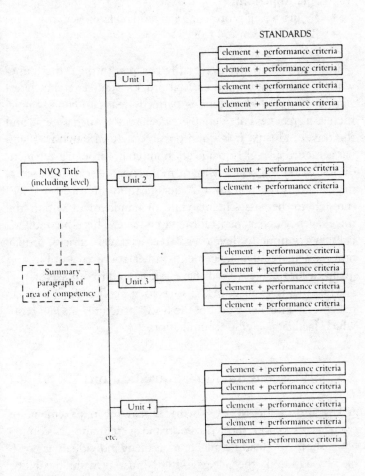

**Figure** 2.3 *NVQ structure*

*Source:* NVCQ 1988a

Progression through the NVQ framework can be seen as an incremental development. Increments will take different forms in different occupational areas. This is because individuals are able to increase their competence in a number of ways:

- By increasing the range of work-related activities they are able to perform
- By mastering more complex work-related activities
- By specialisation.

Individuals may not necessarily progress through the framework in a straightforward vertical order – some lateral progression, across related sectors, is perfectly feasible. For example, there is a great deal of overlap between sectors such as retail and the travel industry. It is quite possible that an individual who has achieved a level 1 qualification in retail, through assessment during work as a retail assistant in a general department store, might progress to a level 2 qualification in travel services through further assessment while in employment within the travel agency department of the same store. This same individual may continue to develop a career in travel services, or may move on in retail management. Either route is possible and qualifications achieved will have relevance in both sectors.

This dual relevance, or 'cross-sectoral applicability', is made possible by a further aspect of the NVQ structure – its *unit basis*, which facilitates credit accumulation.

## 2.3 NVQs and traditional qualifications

A key aim of the NCVQ's work is that the requirement for open access to both the acquisition and accreditation of competence should be made available to as many individuals as possible. In addition, the access system must provide flexibility: modes, locations, entry requirements and timescales of learning should not restrict such access.

As noted in Chapter 1, traditional qualifications are tied to a specific course of study and require a set time commitment and set assessment methods, usually involving study at a specified centre. There are also often conditions of entry to study, such as age limits or previously acquired qualifications.

Qualifications are traditionally, therefore, only available if an individual is able to overcome certain barriers or restrictions to access.

## 2.4   Credit accumulation

Traditional qualification barriers to access include:

- age
- time-based study
- location of study
- specified course of study
- specified assessment methods.

Traditional qualifications are awarded 'en bloc' – individuals obtain the whole qualification or nothing at all. As new NVQs operate on a credit accumulation basis, each qualification is comprised of a number of units of competence, and each unit is independently achievable and separately certificated (see Figure 2.4). Individuals are therefore able to achieve a full qualification by achieving *one unit at a time*. Units can be collected over time, each unit being assessed in the workplace and therefore relating directly to the individual's current work role.

While traditional routes of study (and routes to qualifications) will still be available, and indeed encouraged, the introduction of NVQs means that this traditional mode of accreditation will no longer be the only means available. Widening of access to assessment, removal of time-based study and the introduction of assessment in the workplace have removed restrictions which prevented a wide range of individuals from achieving formal recognition for their skills.

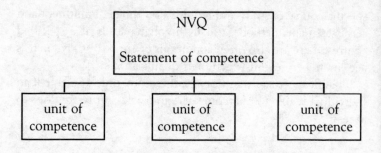

*NVQs are not linked to any specified course of study, nor are they time-based; candidates achieve units at their own pace, the primary form of assessment is observation of performance in the workplace and there are no restrictions of age, previous qualifications etc., regarding access to assessment.*

**Figure 2.4** *Unit-based structure*

## 2.5   Who awards NVQs?

The NCVQ is not an awarding body, it is an accrediting body. It thereore approves qualifications which meet its published criteria (see Part III). The NCVQ covers only England and Wales; in Scotland, Scottish Vocational Qualifications (SVQs) will be awarded by Scotvec (the sole awarding body in Scotland) who have agreed to work with the NCVQ to ensure commonality of standards in the UK.

The traditional awarding bodies – City and Guilds, RSA, BTEC, Scotvec, ITD, professional bodies and so on – will still award national qualifications. They will also submit those qualifications which meet the NCVQ's criteria to the NCVQ for approval as an NVQ.

Awarding bodies have been involved in the development of national standards and have reviewed and restructured their own awards as a result of the changes that have been taking place. As the key to NVQs is assessment, the modes and methods of assessment used by awarding bodies have also been

UNIT STRUCTURE OF AN NVQ

*ABSDA – ASSISTING IN A DENTAL SURGERY*

Statement of Competence (NVQ)
*Assisting in a Dental Surgery*

Units of Competence

1. Control Infection in dental surgeries
2. Prepare for and assist during dental treatment
3. Prepare and select instruments/equipment for dental procedures
4. Select, prepare and maintain materials and medicaments for dental procedures
5. Prepare for and assist in general anaesthesia and sedation
6. Assist with dental radiography
7. Assist in dental and medical emergencies
8. Demonstrate oral hygiene to patients
9. Maintain and control stock and equipment
10. Receive and advise expected and unexpected callers
11. Assess, receive and record payments
12. Contribute to the administration of the organisation.

**Figure 2.5** *Example unit structure*
Source: *Occupational Standards for Dental Surgery Assistants*, NCVQ R&D Report no.1 December 1989.

reviewed. Assessment of actual performance in the workplace necessitates change in the role of awarding body assessors and moderators. Credit accumulation requires a change in the structure of national qualifications. Competence-based standards defined by industry have to be used as the basis for all qualifications which are to be submitted to the NCVQ.

Some Industry Lead Bodies have decided to work with existing validating and examining bodies to become 'joint awarding bodies'. For example, the Hotel and Catering Training Company is a joint awarding body with City and Guilds and BTEC for NVQs in their industry.

It is important to recognise that the NCVQ itself is *not* an awarding body. It approves qualifications which meet its criteria. (Criteria for approval of NVQs is included in Part III.) Your employees will still, therefore, be certificated by a familiar examining or validating body, but if the particular qualification they achieve has been approved as an NVQ, the certificate will include the NCVQ seal of approval in addition to the awarding body's title.

An example certificate is shown in Figure 2.6.

## 2.6 Who develops NVQs – and how?

Chapter 1 outlined the government directives which led to the then Manpower Services Commission (now Training Agency)[1] responsibility for the standards programme and to the establishment of the NCVQ. The same section also briefly reviewed the establishment of Industry Lead Bodies and the arrangements for funding these bodies to undertake development of standards within their industry sectors.

Whilst Industry Lead Bodies (ILBs) have overall responsibility for development of standards and NVQs within their sectors, the actual development must be undertaken *by industry itself*. Each ILB manages a project in which experts from the industry work with a technical consultant to define competence-based standards.

Once the standards are developed, they are circulated throughout the industry, often with a questionnaire, or in test-bed sites to ascertain whether they have real meaning for users and whether they actually reflect workplace practice.

The development of competence-based standards can be a lengthy process, particularly in large, complex sectors of indus-

 **City and Guilds**
of London Institute

National Vocational Qualification

This Certificate
is awarded to

The holder has one or more formal Records of Achievements
by which this Certificate was earned

Awarded

John A Barnes
*Director-General*
*City and Guilds of London Institute*

*Hann Goldsboro*
*Director of Training and Development*
*Hairdressing Training Board*

The City and Guilds of London Institute is incorporated by Royal Charter and was founded in 1878

**Figure 2.6** *An NVQ certificate*

try where many organisations have interest in 'owning' the development process. Where no established Industry Lead Body exists, one has to be set up. This can involve long negotiations with industry training organisations, employers associations, voluntary bodies, trades unions, professional bodies and so on.

The complexities of the standards development programme are illustrated in Table 2.1 which outlines the stages involved in reaching a final draft of competence-based standards for one sector of industry.

**Table 2.1** *Defining competence-based standards*

| Action required | |
|---|---|
| Identify gaps in NVQ framework – which industries do not yet have NVQs? | Training Agency (TA) |
| Identify/set-up Industry Lead Body (ILB) | TA |
| Agree ILB action plan | ILB |
| ILB completes occupational mapping to identify key work roles within its sector | TA/ILB |
| Functional analysis to 'unit of competence' level completed by ILB with help of technical consultant | TA/ILB |
| Standards of competence defined for each unit | ILB/TA |
| Standards verified by industry through consultation process | ILB/TA |
| Refinement of standards based on feedback from industry | ILB/TA |
| Units of competence grouped to meet industry requirements (basis of industry's NVQ framework established) | ILB/TA |

In large sectors, the ILB may need to establish its own NVQ framework. This framework would illustrate how the standards had been incorporated into NVQs at various levels (see the NVQ framework on pp 33–34), and would also demonstrate various progression routes.

Once testing of standards is complete, work continues on the development of an associated assessment system and procedures for maintenance of standards (quality control mechanisms).

Involvement of and negotiations with relevant awarding bodies are undertaken to establish quality control and certification procedures and again, the assessment system is tested within the industry. This process is illustrated in Table 2.2.

**Table 2.2** *Designing competence-based assessment*

| Action required | |
|---|---|
| Determine modes of assessment | ILB/Training Agency (TA) |
| Develop assessment procedures | ILB/TA/NVQ |
| Develop recording procedures | ILB/TA/NVQ |
| Test assessment model and procedures in industry | ILB/TA |
| Refine assessment model and procedures as necessary | TA/ILB |
| Design unit certificate and NVQ certificate | ILB/TA |
| Negotiate quality control procedures with awarding body (ies) | ILB/TA |
| Determine criteria for approval of assessment centres | ILB/TA/NCVQ |
| Determine arrangements for approval of assessors | ILB/TA/NCVQ |

When all consultation and negotiation are complete, the entire package of standards, assessment and certification is submitted to the NCVQ by the awarding bodies for approval.

Links with related industry sectors will also be established and transfer of relevant credits (units of competence) between related sectors will be agreed.

The development process involves the use of a functional approach rather than an analysis of tasks or skills. By identifying the key functions, working top-down from sectoral to individual level, a broader view of work activity (and therefore competence) is obtained. This broad view of competence is represented in Figure 2.7.

Tasks

Task management

Contingency management

Role/job environment

**Figure 2.7** *Components of competence*

In this way, the resulting standards do not simply reflect the basic tasks that individuals and organisations undertake, nor do they reflect 'jobs' (many of which can have the same title but differing content or vice versa). An emphasis on *functions* should lead to standards which provide a realistic and explicit definition of *work roles*. Examples of the standards developed in this way are given in the next chapter.

## 2.7 Implications of the new structure

These radical changes obviously have enormous implications for both providers and users of vocational qualifications. Changes in the assessment process, the removal of mandatory links to specified training programmes, the removal of barriers to access and the abolition of time-based study all lead to increased potential flexibility; they also require fundamental changes in the approach to training, development and assessment.

For *providers*, these changes mean that methods and modes of training delivery must undergo complete review. Closer liaison between providers and employers is required. New methods of delivery and a complete revision of curriculum are needed if the qualification support system is to operate on a credit-accumulation basis. Arrangements for continuous assessment and for recording of achievement must also be put in hand.

For *employers*, the potential is enormous for flexibility of training and development provision, increased cooperation and involvement with providers, better targeted training and performance assessment, improved recruitment, selection, and manpower planning, and ultimately, improved economic performance.

To achieve this potential, however, employers must be prepared to invest in the establishment of work-based assessment systems and the maintenance of quality standards of performance.

Companies are finding that the lead time for introducing competence-based standards and NVQs is longer than the original estimates. Changing the system requires a complete plan for staff briefing and training of assessors as well as a possible review of all in-company training.

For *individuals*, guidance has to be provided on the availability and applicability of NVQs and the units of competence of which they are comprised. Once individuals have identified units of competence relevant to their particular needs, further guidance on suitable programmes of development and progression routes will also be required.

These implications, with their inherent challenges and benefits, are examined in more detail in the following chapters.

1. On 6 November 1990 the Training Agency (TA) was fully assimilated into the Training, Enterprise and Education Directorate (ED TEED). Any reference to the future work of the TA should be taken to refer to the ED TEED.

Chapter 3

# A New Kind of Standard

## 3.1 A foundation for competence

Chapter 1 began with a brief overview of challenges facing the UK and of the new strategy for meeting those challenges which was based on 'standards of a new kind'.

Currently, standards of performance are perhaps the major area of interest to employers. Standards reflect what actually happens in the workplace – and what happens in the workplace affects productivity and profitability. (Qualifications are important to employers for other reasons; we will examine the pros and cons of this issue in the next chapter.)

Also in Chapter 1, you were asked to consider a number of questions relating to the standards currently in use in your own organisation. To refresh your memory, these questions were:

- Who are the gatekeepers of standards for occupational performance of your workforce?
- Where are these standards?
- Are they accessible to all staff?
- Are they explicit?
- Do they represent expectations of performance or do they reflect what people need to know?

For many years, there has been a general concern about Britain's performance in the economic market. This concern is manifest in the enormous interest in the introduction of in-company schemes relating to total quality and the accreditation of companies to meet BS5750 quality assurance.

This emphasis on quality relates directly to the performance of each individual employee.

When recruiting and selecting staff, no doubt you have some form of job and person specification from which to develop a profile of the sort of person you are looking for. For some employers, experience is a key issue; for others, qualifications are high on the priority list.

Many job descriptions and most of the UK vocational qualifications, as well as the education and training system, have not been based on *specification or achievement of precise standards*. As a result, industry has been disappointed in both the quality and actual performance of its recruited employees.

If, as is traditionally the case, standards are based on inputs or what has to be learned, and assessment is biased towards testing of what people know (as in course assignment and examination), it is not surprising to find that actual performance in job roles falls short of expectations and requirements.

However, if standards were based upon expectations of performance, set by industry, and linked to qualifications which could only be achieved through *actual demonstration of the required performance*, then quality of recruitment, selection and actual workplace activity should improve.

The development of nationally agreed standards of competence provides a benchmark for performance across all occupations, provided that industry is fully involved in the development and consultation processes. This was the basic philosophy behind national developments relating to standards (and NVQs). However, from the employers' viewpoint, qualifications are not the main reason for having precise standards. A real test of this 'standard of a new kind' would be its applicability and utility across the spectrum of employment practices.

The issue of utility is addressed later in this chapter. First we need to consider what these new standards offer companies and to review exactly what form they take.

## 3.2  What makes the new standards different?

Two key aspects of the new competence-based standards make them completely different from those traditionally used in training, vocational assessment and award of certificates. The first relates to the basic concept of *competent performance* and has already been outlined: *competence-based standards reflect expectations of workplace performance; competence-based standards express **outcomes** of workplace activity.*

The second key aspect is one which offers considerable potential for future training, development and assessment plans. It is also one which many people fail to grasp – mainly because it requires a complete shift of thinking. Unlike traditional, curriculum-based (input) standards, which are linked to a specific training or learning programme, (and also linked to predefined forms of assessment), new competence-based standards are *completely independent* of both training and assessment processes (see Figure 3.1).

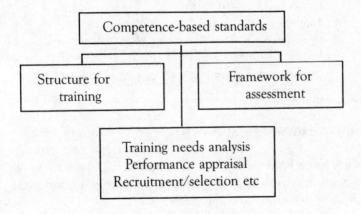

**Figure 3.1** *Independence of competence-based standards*

Because the 'new kind of standard' is focused entirely on required performance, (including the application of underpinning knowledge and understanding), it provides a foundation on which training programmes, 'and/or assessment processes can be developed.

### 3.3 What do these differences mean for my company?

Discussions with a range of employers lead to one key answer to this question – *flexibility*.

As the new forms of standards are completely independent of training and/or assessment systems, (although they are integral to assessment leading to NVQs), their potential use at organisational level is enormous. The last two sections of this chapter provide some stimulus for thought on this issue.

Organisations which have introduced competence-based standards have recognised the benefits of having explicit statements of performance available to all staff. Some of the benefits include:

- staff know exactly what is expected of them
- assessment to specified standards means training needs can be easily identified
- training can be targeted to real needs
- as standards are not linked to any particular training or learning programme, both in-company and external training can be used as well as a wide range of training methods.

### 3.4 Standards and NVQs

New National Vocational Qualifications (NVQs) use nationally agreed standards of competence as the framework for *assessment* of occupational competence.

One of the most difficult concepts for many individuals to grasp was outlined in Chapter 1:

**NVQs have nothing whatsoever to do with training or learning programmes**

If your company introduces NVQs, therefore, it is not introducing a new training programme, it is introducing a new form of assessment of occupational competence which leads to the award of a National Vocational Qualification. Issues of competence-based assessment are outlined in Chapter 4.

The structure of an NVQ was illustrated in Chapter 2, (see p 35). The foundation stones of all NVQs are competence- based standards, the basic composition of which is

- element of competence
- range statement
- performance criteria.

## Elements of competence

An element of competence is a description of something which a person who works in a given occupational area should be able to do. It reflects action, behaviour or outcome which has real meaning in the occupational sector to which it relates. For example:

- create, maintain and enhance effective working relationships (management competences)
- inform customers about products and services on request (financial services competences).

The issue of being *outcome-based* is of prime importance. This represents a strong shift away from traditional standards which are based on inputs or curriculum (ie, what has to be learned).

## Performance criteria

Performance criteria are statements by which an assessor judges the evidence that an individual can perform the workplace activity specified by the element of competence. In effect, the

51

performance criteria enhance the element of competence by stating explicit measures of outcomes. For instance, the performance criteria in Figure 3.2 refer to qualities of the 'objectives' which are to be set by the individual. The 'objectives' themselves are the *outcome* of this activity.

Performance criteria consist of a short sentence with two components – a critical outcome and an evaluative statement (how the activity has resulted in the required result).

## Range statement (and range indicators)

Range statements describe the limits within which performance to the identified standards is expected, if the individual is to be deemed competent.

Range indicators serve the same purpose but some words of caution are relevant. There are two reasons why range indicators rather than range statements may be found in published national standards:

- Range indicators are often developed as the first attempt at defining more explicit range statements. The presence of 'range indicators' may, therefore, suggest that further development work is being undertaken at national level.
- In 'generic' occupational areas (such as management or training, which operate across all industrial sectors), it may only be possible to develop range 'indicators'. As these generic standards will be used across a wide range of commercial and industrial sectors, flexibility in specifying the detailed range statement will be a paramount consideration.

A range statement is a guide to an assessor. A judgement of 'competent' denotes that an individual is able to produce the desired outcomes within the requirements of their work role. This may mean that the individual is able to complete the same activity using a range of equipment or materials, or that they can complete a number of activities within a working context, or within a range of contexts.

If assessment of competence is to be realistic, competent performance in a range of equipment, materials and contexts must be assessed. This is where the range statement serves to 'set the scene' for assessment.

To take our Figure 3.2 example, after the range *indicators* had been examined, and range *statements* specified as appropriate, an assessor would seek evidence of objectives having been set and updated for teams and for individuals, for both short and long term, and using both qualitative and quantitative methods of analysis. In addition, instances of objectives being explained verbally and in writing would be sought as well as examples of single and multiple objective-setting.

When using range statements, an assessor will collect evidence of competent performance across a range of activity. Chapter 4 discusses the new forms of assessment and the importance of collecting evidence of competence.

The example in Figure 3.2 shows how these components might appear in practice. It is taken from a 1990 draft of management competences, developed by the Management Charter Initiative.

## Units of competence

When competence-based standards are developed, using the functional approach as described in Chapter 2, the initial analysis provides titles for *units of competence*.

These units of competence represent workplace activity which

- can be undertaken by one individual
- is worthy of separate certification (ie as a 'credit' towards a full NVQ).

Units of competence *are not training modules*. As noted in Chapter 1, NVQs have nothing to do with training or learning programmes. The components of a unit of competence (ie element, performance criteria and range statement) will probably

*Element II 7.1* Set and update work objectives for teams and individuals

*Performance criteria*
a. Objectives are clear, accurate, and contain all relevant details including measures of performance.
b. Achievement of the objectives is practicable within the set period given other work commitments.
c. Objectives are explained in sufficient detail and in a manner and at a level and pace appropriate to all the relevant individuals.
d. Objectives are updated regularly with the relevant individuals to take into account individual, team and organisational changes.
e. Individuals are encouraged to seek clarification of any areas of which they are unsure.

*Range indicators*
Objectives are all operational objectives within the line responsibility of the manager.

Objectives apply to team, individuals and the manager him/herself.

Objectives are:  short term
                 long term
                 single
                 multiple.

Setting and updating of objectives involve methods of analysis which are:  quantitative
                                                                           qualitative.

Objectives are explained:  verbally
                           in writing.

**Figure 3.2** *Example showing element of competence, range statement and performance criteria*

form the structure on which a training programme will be based, but a unit of competence reflects what has to be achieved in the workplace. It is expressed as an *output* of activity. No sequence of learning or learning input is specified – this is an issue for individual employers to determine when deciding on training needs.

Each unit of competence has three components:

- *Unit title*: this refers to the area of competence covered by the unit. A unit title should not refer to a specific *job*.
- *Description of the unit's purpose*: this is not mandatory, but is sometimes added to supplement the title and possibly describe the unit's relationship to other units within the NVQ. For example, a unit on health and safety may be a prerequisite for units involving the use of machinery.
- *Competence-based standards*: elements of competence, range statements and performance criteria form the standards of occupational competence which reflect the expectations of performance.

The example from MCI management in Figure 3.2 demonstrates what these standards look like. The following sections briefly explain the components of standards and relate each component to its use within a business environment.

Further examples of standards can be obtained from Industry Lead Bodies.

## What about knowledge?

This is a question frequently asked about the new competence-based standards – an understandable question when it appears that the focus is totally on performance in the workplace. Those of us who are familiar with assessment processes within traditional qualifications will be aware that there is a 'knowledge bias' within testing procedures.

A common complaint from employers in the past has been that 'qualified people', although recruited on the basis of having achieved a relevant qualification, still need considerable training because 'they know what to do but have little experience of actually doing it'. A valid concern about new forms of standards and qualifications, therefore, is that those who have been able to demonstrate *performance* will 'be able to do, but not understand what they do'!

The issue of the role of knowledge and understanding within competence-based standards was debated long and hard with all partners in the vocational education and training system. The original directive for 'standards of a new kind' and for the 'reform of vocational qualifications' stipulated that it was the 'application of skills and knowledge' that was of importance in competent performance.

Initial ideas implied that knowledge could be identified within competence-based standards as 'elements of competence' or 'performance criteria'. However this proved not to be the case. This approach simply encouraged separate treatment of 'knowledge and understanding', whereas the aim was to provide an integrated expression of competent performance.

Through various exploratory projects, it became clear that in some respects, 'underpinning knowledge and understanding' could be *inferred* from performance (ie the assessor, as a person experienced in the particular occupational field, would be able to make this inference).

A further issue relating to knowledge and understanding concerns the question of transfer of skills – application of knowledge means being able to transfer 'what you know and understand' within different contexts, or to the use of different equipment, or to dealing with contingencies. In this respect, the range statement acts as a guide (for the assessor) to ensure that related knowledge and understanding are assessed.

This section has provided a very brief overview of the technical issues involved in the development of competence-based standards. For those who wish to delve deeper into technical issues, relevant technical documents are listed in the reference section.

## 3.5 The uses of standards

Consider for a moment how your organisation currently uses standards – if you have them. We have already mentioned that recruitment and selection may utilise some kind of profile for both job and person. What about activities such as manpower planning, performance appraisal, training needs analysis, or judging the effectiveness of training provision?

How about actions for change? do you refer to standards when considering introducing new technology, or implementing a plan for multiskilling, or restructuring the organisation?

Then there is the question of 'to whom do standards relate?' Do you have standards only for skilled workers (maybe in some form of workshop manual)? Or do you have clear standards for all of your workforce, including management?

The big questions are:

- On what basis do you make decisions regarding the restructuring or reorganisation of your workforce?
- How do you take a 'skills audit' of your workforce?
- What information do you use when making decisions about the recruitment and selection of new staff?
- On what basis are decisions regarding future manpower planning made?
- How do you measure performance?

Perhaps an even bigger question is:

- **how do you define performance?**

We come back to attitudes. Does 'performance' immediately suggest issues at organisational level? Issues of profitability, productivity, competitive advantage in the market place? Or does 'performance' also suggest individual work activity which results in these higher-level measures?

If the latter is true, then you are an employer who has at least considered the importance of the contribution of each member of your workforce to the overall 'performance' of your company. You may well have an appreciation of the key part that explicit, industry-defined standards could play in all employment activities.

Potential uses of explicit standards of performance for all work roles might include:

- identifying training needs within the context of organisational objectives
- designing training programmes
- identifying changes in roles
- planning multiskilling activities
- setting objectives for self-development
- improving performance appraisal systems
- manpower planning.

## 3.6 Contextualising standards

Nationally agreed standards of occupational competence are, as noted at the beginning of this chapter, a benchmark for competence across a sector. In areas such as management, or training and development, or administrative and clerical work, national standards will be applicable across a wide range of sectors.

At organisation (ie company) level, decisions to 'contextualise' standards may be taken. Some organisations may feel that the national standards need to be enhanced in order to reflect the company mission and objectives. Some may wish to incorporate specific company standards.

There is no reason why this cannot be done. If nationally agreed standards of occupational competence for relevant work roles remain as the basis of any assessment process leading to award of NVQs, then additional information can be added to these standards.

Many organisations may already have invested in development of 'company standards'. Again, these can either be revised to a competence-based format, or incorporated into those agreed by the sector. It is likely that companies will need consultancy support to complete this work.

The following case study from British Steel illustrates an approach in which the organisation has recognised the benefits which competence-based standards can bring to the improvement of business performance. British Steel's intention is clearly to develop standards of competence for employees which closely reflect business needs. If the standards match up to those set by external accrediting bodies, employees will be encouraged to seek those qualifications. A key issue for British Steel is to ensure that any management workload relating to meeting the requirements of accrediting bodies also makes a very evident contribution to the performance of the business.

Case study

# BRITISH STEEL CENTRAL TRAINING UNIT

The development of performance standards for all employees has been British Steel policy for some time, and all national agreements and the local lump sum bonus agreements contain joint commitments to the standards-based training approach. Specifically, the agreements refer to the 'establishment of standards of job skills for each job and the required knowledge relevant to the job.' The agreements also pursue 'methods by whch employees can be assessed against these requirements.' A senior management steering group on technical and professional training has been established 'to oversee progress on the establishment of appropriate performance standards and assessment methods to establish competence in respect of all occupations in British Steel.'

The standards are now being clearly stated so that all jobholders know what is required of them and their colleagues.

The users, ie the plant personnel (management, trade unions and workforce), are writing these standards. Draft standards in production, technical, engineering and clerical, administrative and secretarial categories are being prepared, then reviewed by the operating plants and functions and amended until they meet the industry's requirements. They are then published for use.

British Steel has been working to develop these standards for three years. The initial work concerned the production and technical (chemical and metallurgical) areas where, in 1989, a number of units were agreed and published as model schemes. This exercise has continued with the result that units covering clerical, administrative and secretarial skills have been developed and are currently being checked by the industry.

A working party on technical skills is reviewing the technical model scheme and identifying the additional units required. A similar working party on engineering skills is overseeing the production of units covering maintenance engineering skills.

A project to analyse the skills required in production occupations is almost complete. Arising from this, a series of units has been produced and checked by plant management. This work builds on the units which became the production model scheme and will form the basis of all standards for the production occupations. The overall plan is to complete the performance standards for production, technical, engineering and clerical, administrative and secretarial categories in 1991. These can then be used as a basis for NVQs.

More recently, this exercise has been extended to cover management and middle-management occupations and a series of functional training committees has been established, under the overall direction of the technical and professional training steering committee to establish competence standards and performance criteria for these job levels.

As the first step towards the development of a structure of NVQs, British Steel, in conjunction with the City and Guilds of London Institute and other steel industry training organisations, made a submission to the NCVQ in December 1989 for an NVQ in iron and steel production (foundation), level 1. This submission has received the approval of the NCVQ. This notable achievement, the first NVQ to be accredited by the steel industry, was marked by the signing of an agreement between the steel industry, City and Guilds and the NCVQ at a formal ceremony in May 1990. The signatories to the agreement were M W Ballin, Director Human Resources, British Steel, on behalf of the steel industry; L Bill, Assistant Director, Education and Training Services of the City and Guilds of London Institute; and Professor P Thompson, Chief Executive, NCVQ.

City and Guilds is jointly responsible with the steel industry for the award of the NVQ, recognising that one of the methods of acquiring knowledge is by taking the iron and steel production technology course. Some employees will obtain this knowledge by other routes.

If the level 1 NVQ in iron and steel production (foundation) proves to be popular and is welcomed by the industry, then other applications for NVQs could follow. These would cover all the necessary levels for staff, up to and including supervisory levels and manual grade employees, resulting in a comprehensive framework of competence standards and NVQs for the steel sector.

The professional direction and co-ordination of the standards development initiative in British Steel is being provided by the staff of the company's central training unit.

## Chapter 4

# New Forms of Assessment and Certification

## 4.1 What is assessment?

This may seem like a very obvious question, but try writing a brief answer for yourself. When you have completed this, try the following questions:

- What do you know/do about assessment of:
  - your company's performance?
  - your department's performance?
  - your section's performance?
  - your unit's performance?
  - individual performance?
  - your own performance?
- How do you assess:
  - training needs?
  - effectiveness of training in your organisation?
- What measures do you use/your company use to assess all of the above?

Let's try a related area – *certification*. When recruiting staff, do you look for staff with particular qualifications (ie certificates, diplomas etc)? Do you know how individuals are assessed in order to achieve those qualifications? You might also consider what the qualification tells you about the individual?

When you have completed this exercise for yourself, you

might like to try the questions on other people within your organisation and compare the answers.

## Personal perceptions

The term 'assessment' can be interpreted in many ways. If we talk about 'assessment of the company's performance', then we may be considering measures such as profitability, market share, productivity. Assessment of department or unit performance may lead us to talk about 'qualitative and quantitative measures' and discussions about 'objectives' and 'targets'.

Assessment of individual performance, in a company context, usually refers to systems for 'performance appraisal' – which, sadly, are themselves often an annual ritual rather than an effective measure – or the term may be reminiscent of periods spent at an 'assessment centre' where various tasks, games and discussions led to a form of management profiling.

Quite often, 'assessment of individual performance' is also seen as the domain of occupational psychologists with arms full of psychometric tests and personal files.

## A traditional view

Our personal perceptions of assessment are probably shaped by our own experiences of being assessed or assessing. In general, most people's experience of assessment is by formal testing of some kind, whether it be a written examination, verbal report or a form of skills test.

We may all have carried out some form of assessment ourselves, perhaps without even realising – an interview situation is a prime example of this. Interviewers make an assessment (or judgement) about interviewees based on documentation and discussion, perhaps with a skills test thrown in.

Traditional forms of assessment follow a pattern of formalised assessment – and usually have formalised measures to use in making judgements. For example, let's consider the traditional form of assessment for a vocational qualification:

student registers for and undertakes
specific course of study/training

student completes course assignments
which are assessed by tutors
(written or skills tests)

student takes final examination
or presents dissertation/thesis.

Table 4.1 outlines the measures that are used.

Most traditional assessment methods use a percentage pass mark. Most are also *norm referenced*, ie individual results are compared with the results of others based on a 'normal' or expected pass rate. Figure 4.1 illustrates what this actually means in practice.

While a well-designed learning programme aims to provide all the input (often combined with practical experience) needed to cover a specific vocational area, this traditional form of assessment results in a final grading which represents assessment on perhaps only half of the actual skills, knowledge and understanding which is required.

Many education and training providers have moved forward from this very traditional position and have improved collaboration with employers in order to make learning and assessment more relevant to the actual work role. However,

**Table 4.1** *Traditional measures of achievement in vocational qualifications*

| Assessment method | Measure |
|---|---|
| Course assignments | 50% pass |
| Final examination/thesis | 50% pass |

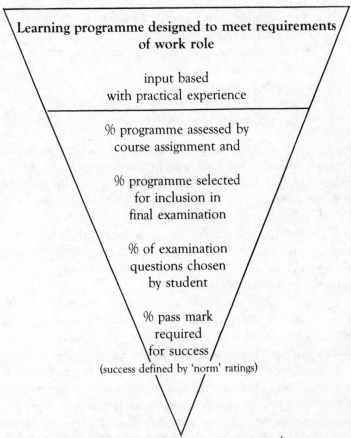

**Learning programme designed to meet requirements of work role**

input based
with practical experience

% programme assessed by
course assignment and

% programme selected
for inclusion in
final examination

% of examination
questions chosen
by student

% pass mark
required
for success
(success defined by 'norm' ratings)

**Figure 4.1** *Traditional assessment procedures*

while percentage pass marks remain there will always be questions like 'In which areas was this individual not assessed?' 'Which areas did this individual choose to avoid in the examination?' 'Were any of these areas critical to competent performance?'

## Competence-based assessment

New forms of assessment (an integral part of NVQs), differ from the traditional approaches in six key areas:

1. a foundation of outcome-based standards
2. individualised assessment
3. competent/not yet competent judgements only (not percentage pass marks)
4. assessment in the workplace
5. no specified time for completion of assessment
6. no specified course of learning/study.

In competence-based assessment, it is *individual performance* which is judged – and judged against explicit standards which reflect not what that individual should know, but the *expected outcomes* of that individual's *competent performance*. How individuals perform in comparison to others is irrelevant.

Only two judgements can be made: either the person has consistently demonstrated workplace performance which meets the specified standards or they are not yet able to do so – 'competent', or 'not yet competent'.

Individuals are assessed in the workplace wherever possible. If assessment is undertaken in connection with the company's implementation of NVQs, individuals will achieve units of competence (and eventually a whole NVQ) at their own pace.

Competence-based standards are available to assessors and assessees. Individuals know exactly what they are aiming to achieve and assessors can provide specific feedback. Assessment on an ongoing basis uses normal workplace performance as its basis, and this continuous assessment process helps in the identification of training needs.

Individuals do not attend a specified course of study (unless the company wish to provide this). Learning can take place on the job, through formal in-company or external courses, through open learning or, indeed, any method which meets both company and individual needs. Training can be targeted to individual needs.

## What is being assessed?

Consistency is of prime importance. A one-off demonstration of skill (as in a skills test) is not sufficient for making a judgement about competent performance. As an employer or manager, you need people who can perform in their work role to a *consistently* high standard.

Standards defined in a competence format, as described in Chapter 3, are explicit descriptions of the expected outcomes of workplace activity. When using these standards as a framework for the design of an assessment system, that framework establishes that it is the outcomes of individual performance that will be judged by assessors.

## Who assesses?

The primary method of assessment in a competence-based system is *observation of workplace performance*. If assessment uses explicit standards of occupational performance as its foundation, then the logical way to assess whether someone is meeting those standards is to watch them working in that occupation.

The next logical conclusion is, of course, that the best people to assess are workplace supervisors or first-line managers – people who have first-hand and regular contact with the individuals who are being assessed.

For those companies who have identified the benefits of introducing total quality management (TQM) and BS5750*, an assessment system which demands involvement of line managers throughout the organisational structure is perfectly in accord with organisational aims and objectives. One can also argue that this form of assessment simply makes explicit what supervisors and first-line managers should be doing anyway.

However, the implications of introducing competence-based assessment (and NVQs) need careful consideration and planning. Guidance on this planning process is given in Chapter 5.

---

* Companies which have been accredited with BS5750 have undergone an audit of their quality policy, systems and control. BS5750 includes quality systems, standards and guidelines that complement relevant product or service technical specifications.

## 4.2 How is competence-based assessment conducted?

We have briefly considered the 'what' and 'who' of both new and traditional competence-based assessment. For most companies who are interested in using new forms of standards and/or qualifications, a prime question is the 'how'.

All assessment is about collecting and judging *evidence*. For the tutor/assessor on a traditional college-based vocational programme, the actual forms of evidence collected are completed course work and assignments and final examination results.

For the workplace assessor, operating within a competence-based assessment system, the actual products of performance provide *evidence* to be matched against specified standards. A workplace assessor will seek evidence of performance which matches the element, performance criteria and range statement for each unit of competence. Where evidence is not available from normal working practice, or would be difficult to generate, the assessor may need to set up supplementary assessments.

For example, a competent worker may be one who is able to deal with a number of contingencies – machine breakdown, sudden changes in workload or priorities, or even a fire. It would obviously not be practicable for an assessor to cause a deliberate breakdown of machinery (or indeed set fire to the building), simply to assess an individual's ability to cope. In this context, therefore, an assessor needs to be skilled in providing opportunities for supplementary assessment. This may involve a skills test, questioning of the individual, or allocating a new task or job.

A workplace assessor requires training in the use of competence-based standards, and in the application of various assessment methods. It is the workplace assessor who 'signs off' an individual as competent, and he/she needs to be confident in this role.

## What about quality control?

Any system of standards will only be as good as the quality control mechanism that ensures they are maintained. Within competence-based assessment systems, and particularly within those that lead to award of NVQs, quality control is a prerequisite to operational approval. For NVQs, various systems are in place, but all follow a basic pattern in which the workplace assessors are supported and monitored by *internal and external verifiers*.

In terms of external quality control the awarding bodies have overall responsibility for assessment within NVQs; they award units and full qualifications. External verifiers support and monitor workplace assessors.

Internal quality control is the concern of internal verifiers – in-company 'countersigning officers' – and workplace assessors like supervisors and first-line managers.

## 4.3 New forms of certification

### What do certificates tell us?

We have already reviewed the traditional pattern of formalised assessment leading to the award of a certificate, diploma, or other form of vocational qualification. At the beginning of this chapter, you were asked to consider a number of questions, one of them being 'What does a qualification tell you about an individual?'

Traditional qualifications usually tell us that the qualification holder has passed the formal assessment process. They may also indicate that the individual has achieved a pass, credit or distinction. This, of course, relates to the percentage pass mark achieved, which, as we noted earlier, is norm-referenced.

### NVQ certificates

Let's consider another question: 'What would a new NVQ tell you about an individual?'

A qualification with the NCVQ logo will tell us that the qualification holder has passed the assessment process. It will not include a pass, credit or distinction grading because for NVQs these grades do not exist. It will also tell us that the assessment process involved assessment of actual performance in the workplace as the primary form of assessment. The certificate will also show the *units of competence* which the certificate holder has achieved.

Now consider an interview scenario. A candidate for an interview presents you with copies of 'credits towards an NVQ'. What does this tell you about the candidate?

Under the new national 'credit accummulation scheme', individuals will accummulate credits towards a full NVQ, each credit being a unit of competence. Awarding bodies will provide certificates on a unit level which can be 'exchanged' for a full NVQ once the relevant total of units has been achieved. These units may be stored in what is called an NROVA.

## 4.4   National Record of Vocational Achievement (NROVA)

The National Record of Vocational Achievement (NROVA) is available to all candidates for assessment leading ultimately to NVQs. All major awarding bodies participate in the operation of the NROVA scheme which is

a common system for recording unit-credits towards qualifications of different education and awarding bodies, in different education and training programmes, in different locations, over varying periods. (NCVQ 1988a)

Roughly translated, this means that an individual can, in his or her own time, collect credits towards an NVQ from a wide range of experience. When he or she has the right collection of credits, they can be exchanged for a full qualification from at least one awarding body.

The NROVA has two main parts:

- Part 1 provides space for an individual action plan (ie the units that the individual is aiming to achieve and a record of progress)
- Part 2 contains the certificates and credit notes issued by various awarding bodies.

Part 2 of the NROVA is divided into three sections (see Figure 4.6):

- the first section will contain certificates or credit notes for units of a qualification which already has NCVQ approval
- the second section will contain certificates which have been issued for qualifications which do not (yet) have NCVQ approval
- the third section will contain certificates issued within certain national training programmes such as YTS, usually in areas where there are currently no national qualifications available.

As NVQs are still under development in many areas of industry and commerce, the qualification arena is in a state of transition. Some newly developed or revised qualifications have already been approved by NCVQ, others are awaiting results of industry standards development projects, and some are not recognised by an awarding body at all.

## 4.5 Benefits of a credit accumulation system (The National Record of Vocational Achievement)*

- Easier access to qualifications
- Units can be built up over time
- Trainees are motivated by immediate recognition of their achievements

* *Source:* NCVQ 1988a.

71

**Figure 4.6**

- Units from different awarding bodies can be brought together in one place
- Integration of different parts of a learning programme and different modes of learning
- Tutors and trainers will be able to operate within a common system
- More flexible learning programmes can be designed
- A clear statement of the holder's competence is provided in language familiar to employers
- It can record credits from one learning programme to another, throughout life
- Acceleration of progress towards a competence-based national system of qualifications.

## 4.6   Conditional accreditation

One further point to note in relation to NVQs is the issue of *conditional accreditation*. When the NCVQ gives full approval to a qualification, this approval is for a period of five years. If, however, the NCVQ feels that the qualification does not yet merit full approval, it will award conditional status, usually for a period of two to three years.

In practice, this means that the qualification does not yet meet all the criteria set by the National Council, who expect that this will be corrected at the end of the conditional approval period.

From an employer's point of view, however, it is difficult to know which qualifications have full, and which have conditional, approval. It is even more difficult to find out what the conditions are!

The NCVQ does publish a booklet called *NVQ Framework – Progress to Date* which lists all approved NVQs by area of competence. It also provides a list of awarding bodies.

Specific information on individual NVQs can be obtained from the NCVQ database. This includes a description of the qualification, who it is for, its level within the NVQ framework, its component parts and what is required in order to obtain it. The database also allows access to individual units of competence so that standards can be examined to find those particularly relevant to specified areas of employment. Information on conditional approval is not included.

For readers who want to know more about this database, details are provided in the reference section.

## 4.7    Accreditation of prior learning (APL)

The accreditation of prior learning (APL) permits the award of credit towards a qualification on the basis of evidence drawn from an individual's past achievements (City and Guilds 1990)

The accreditation of prior learning (APL) is an integral part of assessment for NVQs. It is a process in which evidence of an individual's past achievements within a relevant occupational role can be judged against the standards specified within the appropriate vocational qualification.

Evidence from past achievements must satisfy the requirements of the specified qualification, but can take many forms. Direct evidence of achievement includes 'products' of performance – ie actual outcomes of the individual's work activity. Indirect evidence includes information 'about the individual', such as performance reports, letters from satisfied customers and the like.

The process for assessment of evidence of past achievement differs from any other competence-based assessment only in the preparatory stages. Individual candidates must take responsibility for collecting together evidence which is valid and authentic and matches the specified standards. Initial guidance from a trained adviser will be needed at this stage.

## APL and 'skills audit'

The importance of APL at national level relates to the overall objective of widening access to assessment for vocational qualifications, especially among adults who have a wealth of skill and experience and do not necessarily wish to undertake lengthy periods of study.

The credit accumulation system now being introduced makes the APL approach particularly attractive to a wide audience. If 'credit' for existing competence is available, then education, training and development need be targeted only to remedy gaps in occupational competence.

At company level, this last point is probably of most interest. Better targeted training means less 'downtime', and a higher return on investment in training.

A company's workforce can be awarded credit towards nationally recognised qualifications, without having to attend any form of training or learning programme, purely on the basis of evidence of what they can actually do now. This itself is often a motivational aspect for the introduction of both standards and NVQs, providing benefits for both employer and employees. (Guidance on the introduction of APL is provided in Part II: The Practitioner's Perspective).

APL is now being used as a 'skills audit' process within companies. Between 1987 and 1990 a number of early national projects explored the feasibility of operating APL in conjunction with introduction of NVQs. The Management Charter Initiative is now completing its development project which explores the use of APL with experienced managers. Materials to assist companies with implementation of this assessment process will be available from April 1991.

The final chapter in Part I draws together the concepts, issues, benefits and implications of competence-based standards, assessment and NVQs and provides a checklist of questions you may wish to ask when considering the introduction of standards and/or NVQs within your own organisation.

*Chapter 5*

# *Key Questions for Decision-Making*

This chapter provides guidance and stimulus for thought for employers, managers and trainers who are considering the introduction of competence-based standards and NVQs. It assumes that readers are familiar with the key concepts and operational requirements of these new trends in assessment and certification.

To aid you in the decision-making process, key questions, relating to the introduction of competence-based standards and new NVQs provided in a hierarchical order. These questions are:

- Should we introduce standards and NVQs?
- How do we start?
- What needs to be done?
- How we will use standards throughout the company?

There are no model answers, each company will need to make their decisions based on:

- management understanding of the new structure of standards and NVQs
- the perceived benefits of implementation
- consideration of the key issues involved, including resource and cost implications.

The first of these requirements for decision-making can be achieved by reference to Chapters 1–4 of this book. Readers may wish to refer back to appropriate sections for clarification of specific points.

Guidance on the remaining two is included in the following text. Further information on operational issues is provided in Part II, with relevant information sources in Part III. Readers may also find the case studies of organisations currently involved in the introduction process to be a useful reference source.

## 5.1 Does my company need competence-based standards and NVQs?

**Potential benefits – competence-based standards.**

- Staff will know exactly what is expected of them in terms of outcomes of performance
- Assessment systems (including performance appraisal) can be used effectively to identify training needs
- Training delivery can be targeted to real needs, thus reducing downtime and increasing return of investment in training
- Standards are not linked to any one training/learning programme, so in-company and/or external training can be designed/provided on a completely flexible basis
- Standards will be accessible by all staff, so continuous assessment can be conducted
- Supervisors and line managers can all become involved in ongoing workplace assessment
- Training programmes can be designed, using the standards as the basic design structure, thus making programmes relevant to work roles and more focused on learning which can be put into practice in the workplace
- Standards in competence-based format provide an objec-

tive way of looking at current and future manpower needs

- Standards can be used as a basis for recruitment specifications and structuring of interview questions
- Standards would provide consistency and quality and would contribute to the implementation and achievement of BS5750 (see p 67) and/or the introduction of total quality management (TQM).

## Potential Benefits – NVQs

- External recognition for employees
- Workplace assessment by in-company staff – all supervisors and first-line managers involved in day-to-day assessment of performance
- Meets requirements for operation of YTS and other government programmes in providing access to NVQs
- Company assessment and career planning can be linked to progressive structure of national qualifications
- Employees can achieve qualifications without having to attend lengthy periods of study
- Workplace assessment contributes to more effective identification of training needs
- Flexibility of training provision – the company can design its own training programmes, or use external providers who can provide training which is based on the specified standards
- Assessment of evidence of prior achievements can provide employees with credit towards a qualification and therefore recognition for their existing competence
- More effective links with training and education providers can be made with external provision being matched to both company and individual needs.

## General guidance

The issue of standards of performance has been the basis of considerable debate and development in the last decade. Many companies have undertaken work to develop their own standards. When considering whether to introduce national standards, a key point to keep in mind is that national standards of occupational competence provide a *benchmark across the sector*.

Using national standards within the company provides a basis for *consistency*, not just within your own organisation, but in other organisations across the sector. There is no reason why you should not 'enhance' national standards to incorporate your own company standards, but if you want to provide access to NVQs for your employees, you must ensure that the core of nationally agreed standards remains intact.

Once the system of NVQs has been operational for some time, it is expected that recruitment will be facilitated. Units of competence and NVQs will provide the currency by which employers will be able to identify what potential employees can do and in which areas they will need further development.

The issue of increased flexibility was outlined earlier (see pp 45, 50 and 73). This is perhaps one of the key benefits for employers who can use competence-based standards as a foundation for cost-effective training needs analysis and total flexibility in delivery of training.

## Strategic issues – should we introduce standards and NVQs?

- In what ways do we perceive that the introduction of competence-based standards would contribute to improvement of company performance?
- Are we introducing BS5750 and/or TQM? How would introducing competence-based standards fit in with these plans?
- How would these changes affect job roles and responsibilities?
- Would the introduction of NVQs conflict with any existing company qualification or incentive scheme?
- Do we already have company standards? If so, how will these integrate with national competence-based standards for relevant occupations?

- Which issues need to be discussed fully with trades unions?
- What initial costs (ie registration fees etc) are payable to Lead Industry Bodies and/or awarding bodies?
- What other costs are involved?

## Strategic issues – general guidance

*Improvement of company performance*
This issue must be decided on an in-company basis. A clear understanding of the new structure of standards and NVQs, and of their potential use within an organisation, is essential if informed decisions are to be made.

*BS5750 and TQM*
It is likely that competence-based standards will provide a complementary approach to the introduction of quality systems. New standards focus on outcomes of performance and on improving quality of individual contributions to company success.

*Job roles*
If explicit, accessible standards are to be introduced, one assumes they will be used to assess performance and not just to inform individuals of what their performance should be! This has implications for job roles. Who assesses? What extra responsibility/workload is this likely to create? (It should be minimal if a quality recording system is used. Standards should make explicit what line managers and supervisors are doing on a daily basis.)

*Existing company qualifications/incentive schemes*
If your company already operates an in-company certificate scheme, and particularly if this is linked to some form of incentive or bonus scheme, then you will need to consider how the introduction of NVQs fits in with these arrangements. Even if you are not currently operating such schemes, the issue of incentive/reward needs consideration – people's expectations may well link achievement of qualifications to promotion or other rewards.

*Existing company standards*

Your existing standards may be in a competence format or in some form of 'profile'. It is important to be clear about any differences between your existing standards and those which form the basis of NVQs (ie national competence-based standards). There is no reason why you cannot enhance or 'contextualise' national standards to meet organisational needs, but if you wish to retain the link with award of NVQs, the core of national standards must remain. In addition, simply adding on standards in another format may directly affect the assessment scheme. It is likely, therefore, that you will need some help in integrating company and national standards – or indeed 'contextualising' national standards for company use.

*Trades unions*

National standards have been developed by industry. Trades unions are usually fully represented on the development projects. However, some issues may arise which can be dealt with by careful planning. For example, the question of assessors (first-line managers) being responsible for 'signing off' individuals as competent can be the cause of concern in some areas – particularly in those occupations where health and safety are priorities. Similarly, any changes in job roles may need full discussion with relevant Trades Unions.

*Initial costs*

For some NVQs, the awarding bodies (sometimes Lead Industry Bodies as joing awarding bodies), charge an initial registration fee for 'centres' operating NVQs. (A centre can be a company or regions of a company for example.) Other implementation costs will include staff time for briefing/training and any development undertaken. The initial registration fee usually includes costs of materials, (copies of standards, recording documents etc).

*Other costs*

Other ongoing costs may include an annual registration fee (not all NVQs have this) and certification fees. Two forms of certification fee can be payable – one for a unit certificate and the other for a full NVQ. Unit certification costs vary, but average about £6 per certificate (per person). Full NVQ charges include one payable directly to the NCVQ and are usually around £35 per certificate. If you introduce the use of the NROVA in company, these can be purchased from the NCVQ (cost currently being revised). You will need one for each person registered for assessment for an NVQ.

*Development and implementation costs – general*
In Part II, 'The Practitioner's Perspective' briefly explores issues of whether to wait for national standards to become available or to develop competence-based standards (see Chapter 6). This choice of action has obvious implications for cost. The chart in Figure 5.1 is taken from the Training Agency's *Competence and Assessment* (Training Agency 1988/90) publication and illustrates the key points to consider for development, start-up and implementation of standards.

## Initial planning – how do we start?

- Do we introduce the use of standards in association with NVQs? If not, how will we assess in-company?
- What are the implications of first-line managers becoming assessors?
  - What training will they need?
  - What about legal responsibility for signing off an employee as competent (ie health/safety)?
  - What support will they need?
- What are the key occupational roles in our organisation?
- In which occupational areas would individuals and the company both benefit most from the introduction of NVQs?
- Who are the Industry Lead Bodies in the appropriate occupational areas?
- Are national standards available for these occupational roles? (See Part III)
- Are NVQs available in all occupational areas relevant to our needs?

## [A] COSTS IN DEVELOPMENT

- **costs to the organisation co-ordinating development:**
  (normally an Industry Lead Body)

  * personnel – within the organisation at senior, intermediate, clerical, and secretarial grades, and at technical staff grades
  * staff travel – to participate in meetings, etc
  * internal copying, etc
  * meetings – travel and subsistence of participants catering (whether external or internal) accommodation charges
  * consultants fees – to assist in the proper application of the development strategy
  * printing – to present drafts etc for consultation
  * postage/telephone – for communicating with other participants in the development
  * computer development – any costs associated with developing programmes to record results of analysis
  * computer processing – processing data from development

- **costs to organisations providing 'technical' expertise to the development (normally industry, individual practitioners, ILEA's)**

  * Personnel – within the organisation at senior, intermediate, clerical and secretarial grades and at technical staff grades
  * internal copying, etc
  * postage/telephone – for communicating with other participants in the development

- **costs to awarding/accrediting bodies**

  * personnel – within the organisation at senior, intermediate, clerical and secretarial grades and at technical staff grades
  * internal copying, etc
  * postage/telephone – for communicating with other participants in the development

- **costs to industry**

  * personnel – within the organisation at senior, intermediate, clerical and secretarial grades and at technical staff grades
  * internal copying, etc
  * postage/telephone – for communicating with other participants in the development

## [B] COSTS IN START-UP

  * Same ranges and heads of costs to [A], and in addition to costs under A
  * **NCVQ** – accreditation of award in principle (so, same range of cost heads as for others) apply)
  * **industry, LIB** – training of participants in implementing the system (NOT Training the individuals who will be assessed under the system)
  * **awarding bodies** – participation in training of participants, associated administrative and clerical costs

## [C] COSTS IN IMPLEMENTATION

  * Same ranges and heads of costs in [A] and [B], and in addition to costs under A & B
  * **Industry** people time dedicated to any stage or level with assessment
    - recording with review of candidate performance
    - coping with errors of competence attribution or mis-attribution

**Figure 5.1** *Assessing costs: a) development of standards b) start-up costs c) implementation*

- How relevant are national standards to our work roles?
- Do we want to contextualise the national standards to incorporate our company's objectives or company-specific standards?
- Who awards the NVQs in these areas? Do we have any existing arrangements with those awarding bodies?
- How would we motivate staff to operate to the specified standards?
- Should we consider a phased introduction? Which occupational areas would offer the best test bed site for a cost-effective implementation?
- In which occupational area would we introduce standards first?
- How we will ensure maintenance of standards?

## Initial planning – general guidance

*Can we introduce standards without introducing NVQs?*
Standards have many uses within an organisation, but are of key importance in improving company performance. This can only be achieved if the standards are used within a quality assessment scheme. Providing access to national vocational qualifications may well be a motivational factor for employees and also provides a quality assessment scheme. There is no reason why a company cannot develop its own assessment scheme (particularly if the company is contextualising standards), *and* negotiate approval by an awarding body. This is a viable alternative, but you will need help.

*First-line managers as assessors*
The extension of line managers' roles may have implications which need discussion with trades unions. (See 'Job roles' and 'Trades unions' in the previous section on strategic issues.) Assessors will certainly need training in the use of competence-based standards and assessment. Support systems will also need to be considered, both for the benefit of assessors and for maintenance of standards.

*Key occupational roles*
You will need to complete an 'occupational mapping exercise'. Remember, standards and NVQs are to be available across all occupations of all sectors of all industries.

*Priority areas*
You will need to consider the benefits to both individuals and company based on current operational requirements and plans.

*Lead Bodies*
Part III of this book provides a listing of ILBs and contacts by occupational area.

*Availability of standards*
ILBs will be able to provide this information. The Training Agency (Qualifications and Standards Branch, Moorfoot, Sheffield), also have a database of currently available and soon-to-be available standards.

*Availability of NVQs*
The NCVQ publishes a bi-monthly bulletin of new NVQs and all information is stored on the NCVQ database.

*Relevance of national standards*
You will need to obtain copies of published standards in order to make this decision. Again, ILBs or the NCVQ database will provide this information.

*Contextualising standards*
If you feel that national standards are not entirely relevant, or that your company standards need to be added to this national benchmark, there is no reason why this cannot be done. However, if you wish to maintain access to NVQs the national standards must remain as the core of assessment. You may need help to do this.

*Awarding bodies*
As explained in Chapter 1, our traditional perceptions of an awarding body, such as City and Guilds or BTEC, need to change. Where once the syllabus and examination leading to an award (ie a qualification) were their responsibility, they nowa-

days incorporate standards set by industry into a qualification framework set by the NCVQ. They have overall responsibility for the quality of assessment, but not for assessment methods.

In addition, some Industry Lead Bodies (see Chapter 2) are now also partners in the award structure and have taken on the newly defined awarding body role. NVQs may therefore be awarded by one of the familiar national bodies, or jointly with an Industry Lead Body.

### Motivating staff

You will need to identify the key benefits for each group of staff and consider how you will sell the idea of standards and NVQs. Communication networks need careful consideration.

### Phased introduction

It is probably best to identify priority areas for introduction of standards and NVQs – perhaps admin and clerical staff, or Managers, first, or a key technical area. A clear plan to cover the workforce is essential.

### Maintenance of standards

Qualifications submitted to the NCVQ for approval will have an associated assessment model and quality control mechanism. The awarding bodies have overall responsibility for assessment and quality (as it is they who award the qualification). An awarding body moderator (external verifier) will visit the company on a regular basis (or a sample of companies) to check that the assessment system is operating as it should. You should also consider providing in-company support in the form of countersigning officers (who monitor the work of a number of assessors and countersign completed units of competence). You might also consider regular meetings for assessors to enable them to exchange information and ideas in a peer group environment. This could be combined with, for instance, work on quality circles, or regular departmental meetings.

## Operational issues – what needs to be done?

- Who will be responsible for checking the relevance of

standards to our operations?
- Who will undertake contextualisation of national standards if we feel this to be necessary?
- Who takes responsibility for the planning of introduction of standards
  - across the company?
  - in occupational sectors?
  - in departments?
- Who will be the assessors?
- Who needs to be trained?
- Who trains staff to understand and use standards?
- What lead time should we allow for introduction of standards?
- What lead time do we need to allow for
  - briefing of all staff?
  - training of assessors?
- How much of this time would be allocated to
  - development?
  - training?
  - piloting?
- Who will be responsible for the design of training programmes which incorporate national standards? Do they need training?

## Operational issues – general guidance

*Checking relevance of standards*
You will need to ensure that whoever undertakes this task has a clear understanding of competence-based standards and their use and is also well versed in the occupational area. You might consider workshops of relevant staff led by someone (internal or external) who has relevant competence-based experience.

*Completing contextualisation*
As noted in previous sections, it is probable that you will require external help with this work, unless you have an expert in-house. It is important to ensure that the format of 'enhanced

standards' does not detract from the quality of the associated assessment scheme.

*Planning introduction of standards*
Responsibility for the planned introduction of standards must be allocated to someone who understands what must be done, has the expertise required and is allocated adequate time to control and monitor the process. A hierarchical structure might be adopted with each division or department having a responsible officer who reports to a senior manager.

*Deciding on assessors*
This is a key decision. Assessors must have sufficient contact with candidates to be able to make a fair and confident judgement of competent performance. They must also, wherever possible, be willing to undertake the role – reluctant assessors will not undertake quality assessment.

*Who needs to be trained?*
Anyone who will be using the standards for assessment purposes will need to be trained in the principles and concepts of competence-based assessment, and the use of occupational standards. They will also need to understand the procedures associated with the assessment system. If trainers are to be involved in redesign of training programmes, they will need training in competence-based design. A general briefing and information-providing session for the company as a whole would also be a good idea!

*Who trains staff to understand and use standards?*
As with all training, you have the choice. Some ILBs provide training, some external training providers have expertise in this area. Be clear about the purpose of training: is it briefing on competence-based standards generally, or occupationally-specific training you need?

*Lead time*
This will depend on how many occupational areas are involved in your implementation plan and whether you are planning a

phased introduction. Most companies find that the lead time to actual operation of NVQs is longer than their original estimates. Again, this varies if you are contextualising standards.

*Design of training programmes*
If you plan to redesign your in-company training programmes, then your own trainers will need training in competence-based design. If you use external providers, make sure they can design training to the competence-based standards you are using.

## Further development – how will we use the standards throughout the company?

- Do we have a performance appraisal system? Would we want to redesign this to incorporate national standards?
- Do we have a training policy?
- Do we have a strategic training plan?
- Is our current training plan based on a standards approach?
- Is our current recruitment/manpower planning strategy based on a standards approach?

## Further development – general guidance

*Performance Appraisal*
As you are considering the introduction of in-company assessment leading to NVQs, it makes sense to consider how this links with any existing, or planned, performance appraisal system. This will require a review of the current system and an examination of how competence-based standards of performance can be incorporated into current procedures. You might consider whether formative assessment (ie over time, on a continuous basis) will contribute to the summative assessment (annual performance appraisal and report).

*Training policy and strategic plan*
If you have a current training policy and strategic plan, this will need review based on redesigned training programmes and pro-

cedures which will accompany the introduction of NVQs. With a competence-based system, you will have more flexibility in training delivery: training needs can be identified on an ongoing basis, as part of normal assessment procedures. How will you make best use of this flexibility in your annual training plans?

*Recruitment and manpower planning*
You may want to consider how you can use the standards to redraft recruitment specifications and to facilitate forecasting of future manpower needs. The units of competence will give you a clear idea of the functions carried out in your organisation; this information can also assist with plans for multiskilling or for the introduction of new plant and technology.

## 5.2   NVQs and training programmes

At the risk of labouring a point, it is probably still worth reminding you that NVQs are concerned with *assessment of workplace performance* and not with training programmes.

Many companies, even those who are beginning to introduce NVQs, still ask: how they can get their training programmes accredited by the NCVQ. The short answer is *you can't!*

However, if your in-company training programmes are revised so that they are based on nationally agreed standards of competence, they can, when combined with competence-based assessment, provide *evidence* of competence.

No doubt this sounds very confusing. This dilemma is indicative of the difficulty in switching their thinking to accommodate the new nature of qualifications. You need to keep in mind that NVQs are not training programmes – units of competence are not units (or modules) of training, but units of *assessment*. If your training programmes include assessment of competence (ie performance), then this assessment is providing evidence of competence. You will recall that competence-based assessment requires *sufficient* evidence of competence performance – sufficient for a confident judgement to be made. This evidence will come from many sources, including performance assessed in the course of training programmes.

In Chapter 4, we reviewed the traditional form of qualification. Under traditional rules, training which is undertaken in-company can be reviewed and awarded a 'credit rating' towards a qualification. This system of credit rating does not apply to NVQs.

*Individuals do not simply achieve NVQs simply by completing training or learning programmes, they achieve them by demonstrating competence in a workplace environment.*

## Credit for training programmes

If you wish to arrange for recognition of your training programmes, you can still do so – but not with NVQs. A training programme can be reviewed in order to provide 'credit exemption' or 'advanced standing' (see p 174) in relation to a (non-NVQ) qualification.

This system is popular in the USA. In the UK it operates mainly in relation to degree programmes, but individual educational institutions negotiate separate arrangements with companies regarding a variety of (non-NVQ) qualifications. Should you be interested in following this further, the Council for National Academic Awards (CNAA) or your local college or polytechnic will be able to help.

Case study

# UNITED DISTILLERS – A STRATEGIC APPROACH

The following case study from United Distillers illustrates the strategic planning involved when considering the introduction of competence-based standards and NVQs. It also illustrates how organisations can work closely with awarding bodies in areas where, perhaps, national standards are not yet available, or where specialised interests require a different approach (see Chapter 7).

## Background

United Distillers is the world's most profitable spirits company. During the 1980s it undertook radical reorganisation to streamline operations and restructure worldwide distribution. In 1989 it also introduced a carefully planned range of marketing initiatives as well as engaging in a £100 million expenditure programme designed to improve efficiency, from distillation through to bottling, in the UK.

The company saw the new style of employment-led, competence-based vocational qualifications as contributing towards the achievement of its corporate objectives. A key feature of the company's strategy is a commitment to total quality management in all aspects of its operations. In terms of production, it can be readily appreciated that there are likely to be different practices across a number of sites; difficulty emerges in ensuring quality across the diversity.

One way to overcome this is to standardise techniques as far as possible. The development of qualifications based on agreed performance standards, and monitored by supervisors and line managers, has been recognised as a solution by United Distillers.

## Actions for change

United Distillers began work on competence-based standards with the support of the industry. Consultants were employed to undertake this work and liaison with Scotvec, as the sole awarding body in Scotland, was established.

As well as being an awarding body in its own right, Scotvec is responsible for accrediting Scottish Vocational Qualifications (SVQs) which are analogous to National Vocational Qualifications (NVQs) issued by the National Council for Vocational Qualifications (NCVQ) in England, Wales and Northern Ireland. In this capacity, Scotvec works closely with the NCVQ to ensure mutual recognition of qualifications.

Once standards were established, a major exercise was to brief the workforce and clarify the benefits of the new qualifications. Seven pilot sites were identified and 'road shows' were instigated at each one. Videos and open learning materials for in-company candidates were developed and 'management awareness days' arranged.

Close liaison with Scotvec established an assessment and verification process and also allowed Scotvec to ensure that the company was competent to manage and operate a devolved assessment system across a number of sites.

Training for workplace assessors and internal verifiers was conducted and the overall link of new qualifications to organisational aims and objectives and to individual needs was clarified.

An Industry Lead Body has recently been established and national qualifications, awarded by the Scotch Whisky Association, are planned for 1991. The work undertaken by United Distillers to date will contribute to the establishment of a national qualification framework for the industry.

## Key issues

One of the most important issues to emerge relates to the issue of integration of new developments within the normal working environment. United Distillers endorse an approach which demands careful consideration of the organisation's culture, and the need to be aware of creating an environment of change, particularly one which raises the aspirations of the workforce. The company has invested time and effort in ensuring that new developments become part of everyday working activity, rather than a 'bolt-on' requirement.

Perhaps one of the key considerations for any organisation considering such development is that of cost. United Distillers found that the development and pilot of new standards actually required a substantial investment. However, careful planning at the initial stages ensured that adequate budget allocations were made.

Further emerging issues concern lead time and return on investment. For United Distillers, it took a full year to arrive at a fully operational stage for the pilot, and they realistically expect to wait three to five years before receiving a substantial payback. It is an extremely complex business to implement vocational qualifications *ab initio*, where culture change and training for new roles have to take place alongside other commercial imperatives.

Experience indicates that it is better to overestimate the time involved rather than to be constrained by tight deadlines which might require shortcuts which could compromise quality.

However, the company is pleased with developments and remains convinced that the operation of explicit standards contributes directly to improved performance. They also continue to believe that the implementation of new qualifications, with high-quality work-based assessment, provides an integrated and comprehensive tool in an overall approach to total quality management.

# PART II
# The Practitioner's Perspective: Implementation

Part II takes you through a step-by-step approach to implementing standards and NVQs.

| | | |
|---|---|---|
| Step 1 | Identify occupational areas | ⎫ Chapter 6 |
| Step 2 | Identify standards | ⎭ |
| Step 3 | Collect information on NVQs | ⎫ Chapter 7 |
| Step 4 | Consider implications in operational terms | ⎭ |
| Step 5 | Brief staff | ⎫ |
| Step 6 | Train assessors | ⎬ Chapter 8 |
| Step 7 | Clarify certification of assessors | |
| Step 8 | Train internal verifiers | ⎭ |
| Step 9 | Pilot first candidates/assessors | ⎫ |
| Step 10 | Test recording systems | ⎬ Chapter 9 |
| Step 11 | Monitor procedures and progress | |
| Step 12 | Plan for expansion | ⎭ |

*Chapter 6*

# *Steps 1 and 2: Identification*

Assuming that your company has made the decision to implement competence-based standards and NVQs, your job at the 'hands-on' end of operations now begins.

This chapter provides guidance on taking the first steps, and points you in the direction of collecting the right information, from the right people, at the right time.

So, where do you start?

Logically, if you are going to implement standards, or NVQs based on standards, you must first obtain those standards. To obtain standards, you must first decide in which occupational areas you need them.

## Step 1    Identifying occupational areas

Perhaps your company has already conducted an occupational mapping exercise You may even have clear management direction about which occupations are to be used as a pilot, or as the initial implementation areas. However, let's consider implementation from the beginning and look at what needs to be done to identify these initial or pilot areas.

### What is the key occupation in your organisation?

This should relate to your organisation's *key purpose* or *mission statement*.

The term 'occupation' refers to a key area of work – for example, administrative and clerical, process engineering, management, training and development: all are occupations.

It is important to recognise that occupations, as defined within the Standards Development Programme, may cross traditional boundaries of vocational training and practice. Units of competence defined for a specified occupation may be used in a number of different industries. The occupation lists included in this book are used by the Qualifications and Standards Branch at the Training, Enterprise and Education Directorate of The Employment Department within the standards programme. The NCVQ has a slightly different listing in its database which conforms to the NCVQ framework (ie *industry-defined* standards have been constituted into units with a cross-sectoral usage).

The following list catalogues occupational areas as defined by the Training Agency and the National Council for Vocational Qualifications. This can be used as a checklist for your organisation.

## Occupational areas

Accountancy
Agriculture
Air transport
Amenity horticulture
Animal care
Architecture
Arts/performing arts
Armed forces
Baking
Banking
Basket making
Biscuit, cake, chocolate
Boat building
Blacksmiths
Books
Brushes

Building maintenance/
  estate management
Building societies
Bus and coach
Business administration
Care
Carpets
Caravanning and leisure parks
Cement
Ceramics
Chemicals
Chimney sweeps
Civil service
Clay pipes/refractories
Cleaning
Clothing

Concrete
Conservation
Construction
Cosmetics
Cotton/allied products
Crafts/enterprise
Dairy
Design
Drinks
Dry cleaners/launderers
Education
Electrical contracting
Electrical services
Electricity
Electronic office
Energy management
Engineering
Engineering construction
Engineering/profess.
Envelope makers
Estate agents
Extractive industries
Fibre board/packing
Film making, TV, Video
Fire service
Flexible packaging
Floristry
Food manufacture
Footwear manufacture
Footwear repair
Forensic science
Forestry
Fresh produce
Furniture
Gamekeeping/fish husbandry
Garden/agric. machinery
Gas

Glass
Guidance/counselling
Hairdressing
Hand/machine knitting
Health and beauty
Health and safety
Horses
Hotel and catering
Housing
Information technology
IT – constructive users
IT – practitioners
Inland waterways
Insurance
International trade
Jewellery
Knitting and lace
Languages
Law
Leather processing
Light leathergoods
Leather – saddle/bridle
Local government
Locksmiths
Management/supervisory
Man-made fibres
Merchant navy
Meat
Millers
Mining (including coke)
Museums, galleries/heritage
Narrow fabrics
Newspapers
Nuclear
Office skills
Offshore oil
Packaging

Paint
Paper and board
Pensions management
Periodicals
Personnel management
Petrol refining
Pharmaceuticals
Photography
Police
Ports and harbours
Post Office
Plastics
Printing
Printing ink
Prisons
Purchasing and supply
Railways
Retail
Retail travel
Road transport
Rubber
Sales
Sea fishing
Security

Screen printers
Shipbuilding
Signmaking
Soap and detergent
Small businesses
Small tool/plant hire
Sound
Sport and recreation
Steel
Sugar
Telecommunications
Textile manufacture
Thatching
Theatre technicians
Timber
Tobacco
Tourism and leisure
Training and development
Wall covering
Wastes management
Water
Wholesale
Wire and wire rope
Wool

The above list includes occupational areas where Industry Lead Bodies (see Chapter 1) have been established. If you are unsure of a direct connection with any of the above, refer to the Lead Body section in Part III.

## What are the key occupational roles within your organisation?

This question may present a little more difficulty, as it requires a shift of thinking. The traditional way of thinking about standards is to relate them to *jobs* – but the same job can have many different titles. In addition, there are many jobs within an *occupation*.

The usual source of information regarding work roles within an organisation is the personnel department. You will need to review the information available – but be careful about using job descriptions or job specifications since these outline individual job titles, not occupational roles.

Examples of occupational roles may include supervisor, technician, operative or trainer.

Remember, when considering key occupational roles, to think in broader terms than the key occupation of your organisation. The key occupation may be manufacturing, or processing, or one of the service industries, but key occupational roles will include the *range* and *levels* of activity undertaken within the organisation.

## What supporting occupations occur within your organisation?

To make sure that you include all organisational activities, don't forget to list the managerial, administrative or unskilled roles that support your organisation's main function. If you work in a very large company, many different roles contribute to effective operations.

## Are you introducing standards across the board or in key occupations only?

Having established a clear 'occupational map', you now need to be clear about which occupational areas to address first. In general, organisations tend to introduce competence-based standards and NVQs in the key occupational areas (and key occupational roles) for the initial, pilot phase. In this way, the contribution to improved performance can be judged directly in relation to key areas of performance. However, supporting occupations can also play a key part in successful performance, and your company's decision will be based on consideration of implications and benefits in relation to operational objectives.

# Step 2    Identifying standards

Once you know the occupational areas in which you will be introducing standards and NVQs, the next problem is *finding* the standards.

Current work on development of national standards is gradually ensuring that these will be available in all occupational areas, but some sectors are way ahead of others. You need to find the answers to two key questions: Are national standards available for the identified key occupational areas? And how do these national standards relate to our needs?

Should the answer to the first of these be no, you then have to consider the following options: Do we wait until relevant national standards become available? Do we start work on our own competence-based standards? Are there draft national standards available which we can use as a foundation for our own developments? If we develop our own standards, how can we ensure that we can still link in with new NVQs when they become available?

Taking each of these questions in turn we'll consider

- how to get information
- what to do with the information when you have it
- implications of action.

## Are national standards available for the identified key occupational areas?

In order to answer this question, you need to check with the providers of national standards – the Industry Lead Body or with the providers of qualifications which incorporate these standards – the awarding bodies. This can be done in one of three ways:

- contact the Industry Lead Body direct
- access the NCVQ database
- contact the awarding body.

You should not contact the NCVQ direct for information on standards.

A full list of current Industry Lead Bodies is provided in Part III, together with addresses, contact names and telephone numbers.

The NCVQ database is available on disc for access through a desktop computer. It contains detailed information on all NVQs including the component units, elements and performance criteria and range statements (see Chapter 3 for explanations of these terms). The contact for obtaining the database is given in Part III.

If standards are still under development, the awarding bodies will be involved in this work. In England and Wales the major awarding bodies are City and Guilds (C&G), the Business and Technician Education Council (BTEC), the Royal Society of Arts (RSA) and a wide range of professional bodies. In Scotland, the sole awarding body is the Scottish Vocational Education Council (Scotvec). Each has a publicity/information section and a catalogue of its qualifications. First identify the relevant awarding body from their catalogue of occupational qualifications and then contact their information office for details. Addresses are given in Part III.

Your choice of approach will depend upon whether your company is planning to introduce NVQs as its key objective, or if your key interest is in *standards*. The NCVQ database lists only those NVQs which have been officially accredited (ie after a contract between the relevant parties and the NCVQ has been signed). If you want to know the current state of play regarding development of standards (which will form the basis of new NVQs), then your best contact would be the Industry Lead Body. The Training Agency (now TEED) also publishes *The Standards Digest* (see Part III for details). This lists current developments in standards and NVQs by occupations and is available to those people involved in the development of standards.

Let's assume that you have identified national standards (and NVQs) through the NCVQ database and/or through the Industry Lead Body. As all national standards are published by Lead Bodies, you can obtain a hard copy of the relevant standards and check their applicability within your own organisation. This brings us to the next question.

## How do these national standards relate to our needs?

National standards of occupational competence are developed to provide a benchmark of competent performance within a specified sector. Some developments, such as management competences or those for the training and development fields, are more 'generic' in nature that is, they are used within a wide range of industry and commercial sectors. However, they will have been developed and tested through consultation with key role holders within defined areas of competence.

A key point about this sector-specific development relates both to mobility and exchangeability of the workforce. By introducing a common standard across each sector (and ensuring that the quality of assessment to those standards is maintained), it should be possible to create an employment environment in which recruitment, selection, manpower planning etc can be conducted on a common basis. Instead of having different standards between regions, or between companies, employers will be able to use the new certification (qualification) scheme as a hallmark of individuals' achievements.

Some companies have found, however, that the benchmark of competence, while serving the 'exchangeability' function quite adequately, is not sufficient for their own corporate purposes. Reasons for this perceived inadequacy include:

- the desire to incorporate the company's mission statement and objectives into operational standards
- the organisation's specific culture
- the organisation's commitment to excellence
- previously specified company standards.

This is not to say that new competence-based standards are not applicable – simply that they may need 'enhancing' or 'contextualising' in order to meet the organisational requirements.

There is no reason why this cannot be done, as long as the enhanced standards use the national standards as a core and retain the same format. Similarly, the associated assessment system must retain its quality and meet national criteria – as well as your company's operational needs. It is quite likely, therefore, that you will need help in achieving this contextualisation. This is a cost implication that must be considered.

You may, of course, decide that the published national standards completely meet your needs, and that you can introduce the units of competence (see Chapter 3 ) as they stand. If this is the case, you are in the lucky position of being able to move forward to the next chapter!

It is probably fair to say, however, that having identified the published standards for relevant occupational areas and roles, some difficulties will be encountered. Some units may be completely relevant while others are not.

There is no reason why you should introduce *all* the units from a defined NVQ. There is no point in trying to assess people in areas of work for which they have no responsibility, interest or even skill. The point of a credit-accumulation system is that units of competence are accessible individually. The NVQ framework will combine a number of units into a qualification. Your company may wish to introduce a mixture of units from a range of occupational roles – and even to negotiate with an awarding body to establish a new NVQ in a specialised area.

Perhaps the best way to illustrate this point is with an example. The feature from Post Office Counters Ltd (p 109) shows how a large organisation with specialised needs is making use of existing published standards *and* meeting its own particular operational requirements.

### What if national standards and/or NVQs are not yet available? Do we wait until relevant national standards become available?

The latter question can only be answered in relation to your company's reasons for introducing competence-based standards.

What is the senior management directive on this issue? How urgent is the introduction of standards? For what reasons?

Much will depend on the current state of play in standards development. You can contact the Industry Lead Body for an up-to-date picture and proposed timescales for production of national standards. This will at least provide you with the basis on which to make an informed decision.

If an Industry Lead Body has not yet been established (this will be mainly in small or very specialised sectors), you can contact the Training, Enterprise and Education Directorate (formerly Training Agency) Qualifications and Standards Branch at Moorfoot in Sheffield for information. The TEED has its own database for progress on standards development. The Qualifications and Standards Branch has personnel assigned to each sector of industry and commerce.

## Do we start work on our own competence-based standards?

You can do so, if the company is willing to invest time and money. You may already have company standards which you feel are competence-based. However, you should make sure you are familiar with the basic concepts and methodology involved in developing national competence-based standards (see Part I), before you make assumptions that your standards are in line with current developments.

The costs of development need careful consideration. Chapter 5 illustrated some of the cost headings involved in the development of national standards.

## Are there draft national standards available which we can use as a foundation for our own developments?

This is quite likely to be the case. The Industry Lead Body (or TEED as above) will be able to provide you with information. You should note, however, that most Lead Bodies are reluctant to release draft versions of standards. This is because of the obvious assumption that providers and employers would use them for development of assessment and training programmes, only to find that the final, published version is drastically different!

You should therefore ensure that any draft material you intend to use has been field tested on at least one occasion.

Should you decide to take the route of developing your own company standards, it is likely that you will need consultancy support. Make sure you use a consultant who is fully au fait with national developments, including the technicalities of methodology. Taking a diverse (if cheaper) route can be less cost-effective in the long run.

**If we develop our own standards, how can we ensure that we can still link in with new NVQs when they become available?**

There is no reason why in-company standards (and assessment systems) should not meet national criteria, provided that careful liaison with national developments is maintained during the development process.

Awarding bodies need to be involved in the development stage; most will work with companies to establish a tailor-made qualification (this is essential in highly specialised areas anyway). For an example of this type of work, take a look at the United Distillers case study at the end of Chapter 5.

As you may have gathered by now, identifying occupational areas and standards is a key activity in the introduction of competence-based systems for measuring, monitoring and rewarding performance in the workplace. If standards are the foundation for improvement of performance then the foundation must be solid before any further action can be taken.

Chapter 7 looks at preparing the organisation. This can only be done when you are clear about the nature of the standards which you intend to introduce.

**Get the standards right before taking any further action!**

Case study

# POST OFFICE COUNTERS LTD

## The Organisation

Post Office Counters Ltd (POCL) is a wholly owned subsidiary of the Post Office Corporation. It provides a unique nationwide retail service from its 20,000+ outlets. It is also the leading provider of benefits distribution, postal services, banking and bill-payment facilities.

In addition to its core business, which includes a range of approximately 150 different products and services, POCL operates three supporting businesses which contribute successfully to overall profitability:

- property – in the main, POCL owns the property of its main outlets, local support operations and headquarters
- cash – over 20p of every £1 presently circulating in the UK crosses a Post Office Counter
- retail – POCL is developing its chain of retail shops within main post offices and its offer of retail products (mainly stationery and associated items plus specialist collector merchandise) throughout the network.

## Involvement in standards and NVQs

POCL was created as a separate business within the Post Office in October 1986 and became a limited company a year later. From the outset, its aim was to develop training to agreed outcomes for all of its staff, focusing first on the major occupations.

A substantial review of its Youth Training Scheme trainees was commissioned during 1987, which was to result in profound changes for the scheme and the organisation of business-based training for POCL. It also heralded the introduction of vocational qualifications. A number of qualifications in clerical, retail, business procedures and computer literacy, each awarded by the Royal Society of Arts (RSA), were introduced during 1988 and 1989.

Some contextualisation of the competences was needed to best meet the needs of the organisation. This was undertaken with consultancy support and agreed with the awarding bodies. The qualifications have since been approved by the NCVQ and approximately 500 trainees have graduated to become Post Office Counter Clerks.

Following the success of the Youth Training Scheme experience, POCL took forward work on new competence-based standards and NVQs with a clearly defined business objective to introduce recognised standards for three key groups of employees during the 1990/91 financial year. The largest group (approximately 13,000 employees) are Post Office counter clerks.

During the latter part of 1986, training arrangements for the group were completely overhauled by the training division of POCL to ensure that:

- each and every counter clerk knew their role and purpose within the organisation
- indidividual training needs could be identified and addressed
- training could be delivered by competent, qualified trainers using a range of media
- the outcomes of this training could be formally assessed by trainers and line managers over time, at the workplace
- a return loop for refresher or top-up training was available.

After nine months of developing and testing, these arrangements were agreed with the Post Office unions with input from business policymakers, local managers, training division and the end-user. The proposals were also ratified by the board of POCL.

A further process of validation of business standards was put into practice. The records of over 250 students were examined by the Post Office Psychological Services Unit and all trainers (60+) were invited to provide input. In addition, line and senior managers were asked to comment. By August 1988, the work was complete and the training arrangements confirmed.

POCL therefore created a system in which training for its major group of employees was based on standards set and maintained by the business and which met operational and individual needs. In addition, assessment was undertaken by line managers and trainers.

## New Developments

POCL was committed to the introduction of competence-based standards and NVQs as it believed the benefits of this approach to include:

- a complete relevance to the individuals' jobs – there would be no overtraining simply to meet the qualifications requirement, as had happened within YTS

- full recognition for the standards of the counter clerk job as identified by the business
- the ability to use cross-sectoral competences which were already available and thus allow for transferability and credibility amongst employers and employees
- assistance with career development, manpower planning
- a shift of emphasis from classroom teaching to individual learning thereby encouraging employees to take responsibility for their own development.

During the spring of 1990, the existing standards for counter clerks were translated into NVQ format to allow for easy comparison with accredited competences from a range of Industry Lead Bodies. POCL then sought a suitable approved National Vocational Qualification.

It soon became clear that, because of POCL's unique position, no single NVQ would meet the requirements of standards for counter clerks. There were, however, published standards and approved NVQs in related areas which were the responsibility of established Industry Lead Bodies.

These identified areas included the Administrative, Business and Clerical Training Group (ABCTG), the National Retail Training Group (NRTC) and the financial services sector (banks and building societies Industry Lead Body).

Research identified nine units at NVQ level 2 which would be applicable to the counter clerk role. This included five from NRTC, two from ABCTG Administration, one from ABCTG Finance and one from the building societies. Initial difficulties in identifying a unit for 'manual balancing' – the accounting process that was, at that time, used throughout POCL – later became irrelevant due to plans to introduce automated tills during 1991. (This is a clear example of standard setting looking to the future rather than just to current practice.)

POCL, at an early stage, recognised its position within the NVQ framework. While in some respects the work undertaken within the organisation may be perceived as unique, overlap with other sectoral occupations such as local authority paydesks, bookmakers, gas/electric showrooms, DSS offices etc (all of whom provide an over-the-counter service), demonstrates that this is not the case. Being a sole organisation, POCL were not in a position, therefore, to operate as a Lead Body, but were willing to invest in development of a qualification which would be applicable within these related areas. Other sectors, of course, may wish to add further 'optional units' in order to contextualise the standards.

# Further work

As has been noted, Post Office counter clerks form a large percentage of POCL's workforce – a fine starting point, therefore, for organisation-wide introduction of NVQs. Further developments will include introduction of standards and NVQs for retail assistants – of whom there are currently 50, increasing to 250 over the next two years. POCL will undertake contextualisation of the Retail NVQ at level 2 to meet this purpose. Clerical and secretarial staff will also be provided with access to NVQs.

Currently, secretarial staff undertake proficiency tests at a central secretarial college in London. This presents obvious difficulties when one considers that POCL operates nationally. Plans for the future therefore include introduction of a work-based assessment system for the ABCTG Secretarial standards at levels 2 and 3, to be in place by the summer of 1991.

Developments for clerical staff present a more difficult problem due to the core of information technology (IT) competences within the ABCTG standards. The majority of clerical staff within POCL do not use computers and the issue is therefore one of relevance. A solution may be found, however, through a 'skills audit' to identify the range of activity undertaken by clerical staff and to match this range to the ABCTG competences.

For junior managers, whose training is currently undertaken in-house at POCL's three management colleges, several possibilities are under consideration. A link with competences defined by the Management Charter Initiative (MCI) is being explored and the provision of access to, or exemption from, current management qualifications, including those offered by the Open Business School, is also a possibility.

## In-company assessment

NVQs require quality assessment of *performance* – and performance is best assessed in the workplace. POCL is therefore addressing the issue of work-based assessment and undertaking a process of identifying and training in-company assessors.

Two levels of in-company assessment are proposed for Post Office counter clerks: the first-line assessor, who must have regular contact with candidates for an NVQ, will be the branch manager. The role of 'countersigning officer' or 'internal verifier' will be taken by the area manager.

POCL recognises that quality of assessment is the key to successful operation of NVQs. It also recognises that there are still many issues to be addressed in their attempts to introduce a high-quality assessment system. The organisation is, however, fully committed to a competence-based approach and plans to use the new form of standards to their full potential. This will include structuring of training and performance appraisal, recruitment, selection and manpower planning. In-company trainers will be trained both in the design of competence-based training and in competence-based assessment.

Case study

# INSTITUTE OF CHARTERED SECRETARIES AND ADMINISTRATORS

The Institute of Chartered Secretaries and Administrators is currently involved in the advancement of a Lead Body consortium to develop specifications for occupational standards across a variety of sectors at professional level as well as the interaction between administration and strategic management.

Work is currently proceeding on an informal basis via general consultation as opposed to specific project work; confirmation of NCVQ policy at post-level 4 is awaited.

In the meantime, the Institute has begun to take forward work in the field of utilities administration and will be piloting two new modules at polytechnics. These modules are the results of lengthy consultations with senior utilities practitioners around the country and represent their endorsement of the standards required at junior/middle management levels in their own sector.

The Institute aims to encourage educational establishments to focus on the ultimate enhancement of job proficiency without dilution of the underpinning intellectual rigour. It also seeks to provide tutors with flexibility in adopting more innovative and vocationally relevant modes of delivery and assessment.

The modules will carry full credit as two job-related subjects in the professional level of the ICSA qualifying programme but will only be assessed via internal means and not by three-hour unseen external examination.

Modification and refinement will be conducted in the light of both experience and changing job needs. Practitioner advisors are being assigned to the prospective delivery centres to ensure that professional and vocational relevance is maintained.

The Institute hopes that in due course, the college-based focus could extend to in-company delivery, hence dismantling any preconceived distinctions between education and training.

While the Institute is fully aware that the two new modules do not as yet conform to NCVQ specifications for standards, their introduction is seen as a step in the direction of competence-based provision for those seeking entry to professional levels.

An example from the Utility Organisation and Management module is given below.

## Utility Organisation and Management

1. *Learning objectives*

   To understand and explain:
   - the internal and external structure and organisation of the utilities within the UK;
   - historic and current factors influencing the development and operation of the utilities sector;
   - emergence of new utilities frameworks and associated management considerations;
   - strategy followed by utilities in relation to their social responsibilities;
   - the legal environment within which utilities are required to operate;
   - the role and impact of government policies on the utilities;
   - the role, accountability and authority of managers and management;
   - the importance of managing change and the means by which it might be achieved.

2. *Competences*

   The Organisation and Management Module is designed to provide a general understanding of the major factors affecting the operation of utilities. As such, it will be a basic building-block for progression into a number of different sections within the company, eg company secretarial office, corporate planning, regulation, organisation and development, accounting functions, customer service.

   Candidates will have acquired a basic understanding of the subject through the Management Principles and Practice core module. Candidates offering the Utilities Organisation and Management Module will therefore be expected to relate their general knowledge to the utilities sector. On completion of this module, the student will be able to:

## ORGANISATION
*Features of utilities*
i)    Analyse the extent to which the key characteristics of utility structures conform to typical organisational models and other aspects of organisation theory.
ii)   Identify the conflicts and dissonance in static organisational structures in times of change.
iii)  Make recommendations as to an appropriate organisational structure for a UK utility.

*Comparative structures*
i)    Identify key differences in the organisational structures of major UK utilities.
ii)   Comment on the merits and disadvantages of the organisational structures of utilities in Europe and in the USA.
iii)  Analyse the similarities and differences between utilities and other major organisations (conglomerates, government, departments, multinationals etc).
iv)   Argue the case for and against organisational and managerial differences between utility and non-utility plcs.

*History of utilities*
i)    Trace the development of one or more major UK utilities, identifying and evaluating differences.
ii)   Set current organisational structures in the context of their historical development.
iii)  Describe precedents which might contribute usefully to decisions about future organisational change.
iv)   Analyse the reasons for nationalisation in the 1940s and the legislative and organisational characteristics it created.
v)    Understand and describe the forces leading to privatisation.

*External influences on organisational structure*
i)    Account for the nature and strength of statutory control over the current structure of a selected utility.
ii)   Assess the likely public reaction to changes in the organisational structure of utilities (eg centralisation, diversification, social and community policies).
iii)  Assess government and public pressure on utilities and evaluate their effects.

*Decision-making processes*
i)    Advise on the political and statutory obligations to be taken

into account when planning organisational change.

ii) Distinguish between the roles of the utility's executive staff and its non-executive members.

iii) Identify factors external to the organisational structure which might influence the course of the decision-making process (eg national pay bargaining, environmental issues, customer attitudes and perceptions).

## MANAGEMENT

*Management style*

i) Assess the relevance of management style to the structure of a utility and the achievement of its corporate objectives.

ii) Draw out the external influences impacting upon the style of management in a selected utility.

iii) Identify areas of potential conflict and recommend changes in style which could limit damage to the utility.

*Statutory accountabilities*

i) Describe the limitations on managerial freedom imposed by regulation.

ii) Advise on the legislative and licensing regimes affecting the management of utilities.

*Social responsibilities*

i) Advise on activities which enhance the utility's community relations.

ii) Advise on laws, statutes and codes of practice affecting the manner in which the utility carries out its activities.

iii) Understand and evaluate the environmental and social dimensions within which utilities function.

*Inter-utility relationships*

i) Describe and comment on the changing nature of the relationships between utility companies providing similar services.

ii) List the benefits and problems of liaison and collaboration with other utility companies.

iii) Compare and evaluate diversification policies.

*Financial accountability*

i) Interpret financial information and describe differences in financial management and outturns in other companies and utilities.

ii) Advise on the constraints imposed by external influences on a utility's sources of income and investment.

iii) Undertake cost/benefit feasibility studies in line with the risk parameters and service standards prevailing in the utility.

*Planning processes*
i) Advise on the regulatory, statutory and licensing obligations affecting a utility's plan.
ii) Describe the differing viability and risk criteria applicable to controlled as opposed to entrepreneurial activities.
iii) Examine the impact of performance criteria on utility management and evaluate the effect on the company's success.

*Source:* Institute of Chartered Secretaries and Administrators, 1990.

*Chapter 7*

# Steps 3 and 4: Preparing the Organisation or Department

### Step 3　　Collecting information on NVQs

Once you have established the nature of the competence-based standards you are going to introduce, you are ready to consider the implications of their introduction.

If you are also introducing NVQs (with national standards as their base) you will be ready to collect information on these qualifications from the awarding bodies, which may include the relevant Industry Lead Body itself (see Chapter 1 and case study on Post Office Counters p 109).

Each NVQ will have specific requirements attached relating to the assessment process. For example, some NVQs (such as those in the hotel and catering industry) have a requirement for workplace assessors to be 'registered'. Some may supply documentation for recording assessment as part of the initial registration fee.

You may be introducing a full NVQ (ie all units of a specified qualification) or units of more than one full NVQ (as in the Post Office Counters case study), but all NVQs will include arrangements for quality control – referred to as 'verification' or 'moderation'. An *internal* verifier is a designated person within the company who monitors the work of in-company assessors (often supervisors or first-line managers). An *external* verifier is an awarding body representative who will visit a sample of companies on a regular basis to ensure that standards are being maintained and that the assessment system is operating as it should.

The costs of verification are often built in to the NVQ operational system. They may be included in an initial registration fee, or in annual operating costs. You should ask for clarification of all costs involved.

'Certification' refers to the award of certificates to successful candidates. This usually involves a separate fee and can be charged on a unit certificate basis (usually around £6 per unit), or on a full NVQ basis (usually around £35 per certificate). You should clarify whether fees include issue of an NVQ certificate. Awarding bodies have their own system of charging for their own certificates, and the NCVQ also have a certification charge.

## What to ask about NVQs

- What are the requirements for assessment of units?
- Are there specific requirements for
  - training of assessors?
  - registration of assessors?
- Is there an initial registration fee?
- If so, what does this registration fee cover?
- Is the registration fee payable annually?
- Is there an 'assessment centre approval process' attached to registration?
- What are verification and moderation arrangements?
- Are there any hidden costs involved?
- What are the arrangements for certification of successful candidates?
- What are the certification fees?
- Is there any separate arrangement for assessment of knowledge and understanding?
- Is there a procedure for accreditation of prior learning?

## Step 4 Consider the implications in operational terms

Introducing competence-based standards and NVQs will have a direct impact on the training culture within your organisation.

Systems of workplace assessment require commitment and involvement. Learning programmes will need to be revised or developed to contribute towards achievement of required standards. Staff will take on new roles and responsibilities – a point to note when discussing changes with trades unions.

You might think of the introduction of competence-based standards and NVQs as a programme for change. Like all change programmes, it will require careful planning to ensure that the staff resources and expertise are available, and that the new actions for change will influence company operations only in a positive sense.

You will need to establish an in-company assessment model. This means considering who will be designated assessors and how they will assess. Who will train assessors and how will they be trained? What costs are involved in this activity? Does the awarding body or Industry Lead Body specify a training programme or can you develop one of your own? Will your assessors gain qualifications in assessment? Is this a requirement?

You must also consider *quality control*. Who will be designated as internal verifier? Who will be the key contact for introducing standards and NVQs? Who will liaise with awarding bodies regarding external verification and certification?

You will also need to consider training implications. Who will be responsible for ensuring training contributes to achievement of standards? When will training programmes be developed? How will training delivery be affected?

If this sounds like a great deal of work – it is! Any programme for change requires considerable effort and it is essential that all roles and responsibilities are clarified before implementation begins.

The checklists below will help you with some of the key questions you need to consider at this vital planning stage.

## Introducing standards and NVQs – initial checklist

Does your organisation have

- a clear training policy?
- a clear training strategy?
- a plan for implementing standards and NVQs?
- a senior staff member designated with responsibility for implementation?
- job descriptions which outline training responsibilities?
- a staff appraisal system?
- a system for forecasting staffing needs?
- an agreed culture?
- existing company qualifications?
- existing reward/incentive schemes?
- existing arrangements with awarding bodies/educational institutions for award of qualifications?
- existing continuous assessment schemes?
- company-defined learning/training programmes?
- company-defined standards?
- selection/recruitment policies linked to job descriptions?

All or any of the above activities can influence, or be influenced by the introduction of competence-based standards and NVQs. In order to understand the implications and benefits on each activity, you must have a clear understanding of the concepts and principles of these new developments, and of the specific operational requirements of the NVQs you intend to introduce.

If you decide you need help to plan the introduction of standards and NVQs, Industry Lead Bodies and awarding bodies can provide guidance. Consultancy help is also available, but make sure you check that your chosen source of help is fully cognisant of developments and is able to consider the application of these developments within your specific company context.

## Introducing standards and NVQs – staff role checklist

*Management responsibility*
Who is responsible for

- implementing standards/NVQs at
  - organisational level?
  - departmental level?
- liaison with awarding bodies?
- monitoring effectiveness of new systems/
- arranging development of competence-based training programmes?

*Operational responsibility;*
Who is responsible for:

- initial assessment procedures (including assessment of prior learning)?
- assessing candidates' performance at work and recording assessment?
- monitoring (verifying) assessors' work including counter-signing assessments?
- identifying training needs?
- preparing training plans?

## Trades Unions

A brief note regarding discussions with trades unions is essential. By now, you are probably fully aware that the introduction of competence-based standards and NVQs can have far-reaching implications and benefits for your organisation.

Not least of these is the potential perceived change in staff roles and responsibilities. For those companies who have introduced total quality management, or BS5750, or some form of total quality system, the idea of line management's greater involvement in the development and assessment of staff will not come as any great shock. In fact, competence-based standards should serve to make explicit what supervisors and line managers are doing on a daily basis anyway – continuously assessing the performance of staff for whom they have direct responsibility.

However, the introduction of assessment recording systems, on an individual basis, is likely to be met by a wide range of reactions that you must be prepared to deal with. No doubt trades unions will want to question the changes in roles and responsibilities – the introduction of NVQs, with external recognition for work performance, is a form of reward or incentive system.

Some of the issues which may arise will relate to existing incentive schemes (or previous ones). Others may relate to the fact that assessors are being given responsibility for 'signing off competence'. This latter issue may be particularly problematic in sectors where health and safety is a key issue. For example, what happens if a line manager/supervisor 'signs off' an employee as competent in installing a delicate or potentially dangerous piece of equipment and something goes wrong with that equipment?

This will be a valid and pertinent point to be addressed in many industries, as will issues pertaining to incentive and reward. But there is no universal guidance on these matters. Careful planning through consideration of all the issues outlined in this and the previous chapter will help you prepare for such discussions.

## Accreditation of prior learning

This integral part of competence-based assessment is covered in more detail in Chapter 11, but needs mention here in relation to forward planning.

The accreditation of prior learning (APL) permits the award of credit towards a qualification on the basis of evidence drawn from an individual's past achievements. For companies, this means that you can use the APL assessment process to take a skills audit of your staff and provide them with credit towards an NVQ as recognition of their current level of competence.

An additional benefit for you is that, having completed this assessment, training needs will have been clearly identified, on both individual and group bases, and future training can be targeted to those areas where it is really needed. This will obviously save time and provide a more cost-effective training solution as well as providing motivation for staff to be both assessed and trained.

The major awarding bodies have developed and agreed policies for the operation of APL in connection with a wide range of qualifications. However, procedures for operating the APL process within all occupational areas have not yet been finalised. You will therefore need to check that procedures are in place within the relevant occupational areas.

The costs involved will include a fee for verification (paid to the awarding body) and training of assessors. Given the overall benefits of operating APL as an initial assessment process, this is a cost-effective means of introducing NVQs.

The responsibility for collecting evidence of competence (to match the specified standards), rests with individual candidates. You may need to allow time for your staff to do this.

Further information on APL is included in Chapter 11; copies of awarding bodies' guidance and policy is available on request from their central offices.

Once again, should you need help to introduce APL, check that your source of help is fully cognisant with the concepts, principles and operational requirements involved.

*Chapter 8*

# Steps 5 to 8: Staff Briefing and Development

## Step 5  Staff briefing

Once you have a plan for the introduction of competence-based standards and NVQs, you need to consider how to communicate those plans to everyone involved.

Much will depend upon your implementation plan, but it is usually a good idea to consider an organisational briefing which outlines the reasons behind the decision to introduce new developments, together with the benefits to both the organisation and the individual.

You might consider using an existing staff newsletter, or networking structures to cascade information. Alternatively, a special staff briefing might be arranged. Whatever your choice, consider the following points for inclusion in a major briefing exercise:

- reasons why standards and NVQs are being introduced
- explanation of what standards and NVQs are
- description of areas they are being introduced in
- details of the order they are being introduced – and why
- how the company will benefit from the introduction
- how individuals will benefit from the introduction
- trade union support
- what the introduction means in terms of staff roles and responsibilities
- when the first implementation will start

- how it will be monitored
- procedures for people to communicate ideas and feedback
- request for applications for first candidates (if you are conducting a pilot scheme first).

## Staff development

Companies have been quick to realise the potential flexibility that competence-based standards offer to the training function. With explicit and measurable standards of expected performance which can be made available to everyone who uses them, the design and delivery of training becomes less hit and miss and more directly targeted to individual and group and company needs.

However, as companies begin to introduce new competence-based standards and NVQs, they are also beginning to realise the importance of staff development, particularly for assessors.

Most of us have a particular perception of assessment. The traditional view was outlined in Part I. If you are unclear about the principles and concepts of competence-based assessment, and how they differ from the more traditional approach, you should read through Chapter 4 before continuing with this section.

## NVQ assessment model

All NVQS operate within a defined assessment model (see Figure 8.1). Assessment is determined by the elements of competence, range statements and performance criteria which form the standards of competence. Assessment itself is a process of obtaining evidence and making judgements about that evidence.

The key form of assessment within NVQs is therefore observation of performance. However, this is not always possible, particularly in the case of various contingencies or health-and-safety-hazardous environments.

Assessors operating within competence-based systems must therefore be fully aware of various methods of assessment and

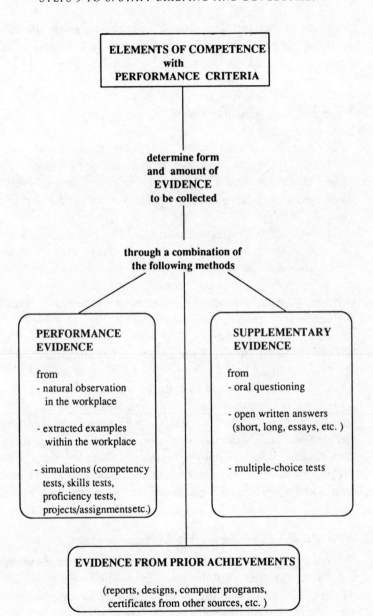

**Figure 8.1** *The NVQ assessment model*

their use within the workplace if they are to assess the full specified range of activities. (Further detailed discussion of competence-based assessment will be found in Chapter 11.)

## Step 6     Assessor training

One particular danger of introducing competence-based standards and NVQs is the tendency to assume that people already know about assessment. After all, isn't competence-based assessment only making explicit what supervisors and line managers do anyway?

This is true, although perhaps it would be more accurate to say that competence-based assessment makes explicit what supervisors and line managers *should* be doing anyway! How consistent is continuous assessment in your organisation? How good are your line managers at recognising and reporting training needs, or completing annual appraisals?

While we may all have a good idea of what assessment is, when it comes to actually doing it we find that our ideas are not the same as those held by the people we have to assess, or by our colleagues who have to conduct a similar assessment.

The point of introducing competence-based systems is to gain *consistency*. Consistent maintenance of standards, both in performance and assessment, can contribute to development of performance. It is important to recognise, therefore, that *training of workplace assessors* is vital to the successful implementation and operation of competence-based systems.

### Training programmes for assessors

Workplace assessors need to be competent in their assessment role. You may find that the awarding bodies for the NVQs which you plan to introduce offer assessor-training programmes. The benefits of these are that they are usually sector-specific and deal with issues arising from the particular NVQ.

However, with a focus on quality of assessors, you should

check that the assessor training will meet your operational requirements and that it includes the following:

- basic concepts of competence-based assessment
- issues of evidence of competence
- assessor skills, including use of various methods of assessment
- maintaining quality of assessment
- procedures and processes for assessment of performance and for assessment of knowledge and understanding (these are sometimes separate, eg financial services sector)
- procedures for accreditation of prior learning, including issues of evidence from past achievements
- verification/moderation procedures
- recording procedures and documentation
- certification procedures
- appeals procedures

You may find that the content or the duration of assessor training courses on offer do not meet your operational needs. You may choose to develop and deliver your own in-company programme, or to use external consultants to do this for you. Once again, the issue of making sure that your selected consultant is au fait with developments and key concepts is a paramount issue.

## Step 7    Certification for assessors

Awarding bodies have overall responsibility for assessment in connection with NVQs because they award the final certificates. You may therefore find requirements for 'registration' of assessors. There may also be a requirement for assessors to achieve a recognised qualification. You can arrange this through liaison with an awarding body (or your external consultant could take care of this for you). This will, of course, involve your in-company assessors undergoing assessment. (The terminology gets confusing – who assesses assessors?!)

This need not be complicated. All your in-company assessors will be monitored by an internal and an external verifier (see p 69 for explanations of these terms). Assessors will therefore be demonstrating competence in their assessment role on an ongoing basis – in the same way as the people they are assessing are demonstrating competence in their work roles.

## Step 8      Internal verifier training

Internal verifiers are in-company staff responsible for monitoring assessment. They may also have a role as 'countersigning officers' – responsible for signing the assessment documentation to support the decision of the first-line assessor. Verifiers will need to understand the basic concepts, principles and procedures of competence-based assessment in the same depth as first-line assessors. They will also need to be clear about the verifier's role and liaison with awarding bodies.

### Accreditation of prior learning (APL)

Once again, a separate note on this issue, although it is an integral part of competence-based assessment.

If you are planning to introduce APL, you will have included training in this form of assessment in your initial assessor training package. It is essential to the credibility of the assessment system that assessors are aware of issues relating to evidence from past achievements and can provide quality guidance to candidates. (A brief discussion of these issues is provided in Chapter 11.)

### A question of choice

When introducing competence-based standards and NVQs, your company can choose whether to use nationally agreed standards of competence as they stand, or to enhance or 'contextualise' them to meet organisational demands. Similarly, you can choose to make use of the assessor training packages available to you or to develop your own. These decisions must be based on a review of the specific NVQs you plan to introduce.

## Chapter 9

# Steps 9 to 12:
# Starting, Maintaining and Expanding the system

## Step 9     Pilot first candidates and assessors

When your initial training programmes are complete, you are ready to start your first assessments. Remember, these are not traditional assessment procedures of a one-off nature, your in-company assessment scheme will operate on a continuous day-by-day basis.

### Briefing the candidates

All candidates for assessment should be fully briefed about the assessment system. They should have easy access to the standards at all times – and to their assessor.

The designated assessor (usually a line manager), who may be responsible for several candidates (usually his own staff), should meet with the candidate and ensure that a clear *assessment plan is agreed*.

### Assessment plans

The purpose of an assessment plan is to set parameters for both candidate and assessor. Both need to be clear on *what* is being assessed and *how* it is being assessed.

As competence-based assessment focuses on evidence of performance, assessor and candidate can decide what forms of evidence are most likely to be created in the normal work pattern of the candidate.

The assessor and candidate will need to agree which *units of competence* the candidate will be aiming to achieve. They can also agree a timescale for assessment. Figure 9.1 illustrates a typical process for agreeing an assessment plan.

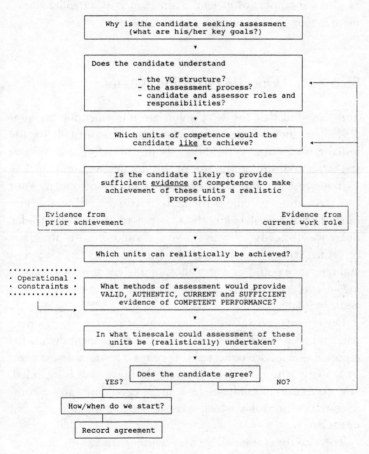

**Figure 9.1** *A typical assessment plan*

133

## Assessor support

Assessors will need support, not only to help them in the role, but also to ensure that standards are maintained. A networking system, allowing assessors to meet on a regular basis, would enable a forum for exchange of ideas and mutual support to be established.

Regular meetings with internal verifiers and external verifiers should also be encouraged. These arrangements will obviously need to fit in with operational requirements, but the importance of assessor support to general maintenance of a quality assessment system should not be underestimated.

## Step 10     Operate recording systems

You may find that the NVQs you are implementing are supported by documentation for recording assessment. If so, the initial introduction to the NVQ, both in briefing and training stages, should outline the use of this documentation.

In general, there is no reason why you cannot operate your own recording system, particularly if you find that the one offered by the awarding body does not meet your day-to-day operational needs. However, you should ensure that any recording system includes clear guidance for assessors (as a general reference point) and also allows sufficient space for recording of evidence presented, and signatures of assessor, verifier and candidate.

Documentation relating to assessment must be kept up to date and available for verifiers to review. Assessment documentation and evidence collected can be used for final assessment, particularly where evidence from past achievement is included. Any collection of evidence by a single candidate can be compiled into a 'portfolio' which serves as an assessment document in itself.

The assessor is responsible for recording the results of assessment. Records should be maintained legibly and accurately and be accessible to candidate, assessor, assessor-colleagues and verifiers. However, confidentiality between candidate and those staff with legitimate access to records must be maintained.

## Step 11    Monitor procedures and progress

The internal and external verifiers will be responsible for monitoring of the assessors and the assessment system. However, maintenance of standards is a key issue for your company – consistency of performance through the introduction of standards is one of the key reasons for introducing competence-based standards.

You may wish to introduce your own monitoring system, perhaps using the external verifier as a source of information, as he/she will have a general overview of the progress of a number of candidates and a number of assessors.

Specific questions you may consider include:

- How is the assessor/candidate ratio working out?
- Are assessors able to cope with the number of candidates?
- Are assessors/candidates having any difficulties with
  - types of evidence required?
  - organisation of workload to produce range of evidence required?
  - coping with assessment documentation?

In addition to monitoring the actual assessment system, you will also want to consider measures of effectiveness as the first part of your evaluation of the new system's contribution to improved performance.

The measures you may choose to use in this respect will be similar to those used to evaluate the effectiveness of training:

- increased productivity
- lower absenteeism

- lower level of complaints
- decreased reject rate.

It is probably a good idea to begin compiling your overall evaluation plan at this stage. By using initial information on progress you will begin to formulate a clear idea of the most appropriate measures to apply.

## Step 12    Plan for expansion

When your pilot programme is running smoothly, you will need to consider plans for expansion. The following questions might be considered:

- How many more candidates for assessment do we have in this occupational area?
- Do we have adequate numbers of assessors?
- How can we phase training of assessors and introduction of assessment across all staff in this occupational area?
- What will be the next occupational area in which we will introduce NVQs?
- Are there any differences between operational requirements for NVQ in the second occupational area?
- What difficulties have arisen in this first area that we can also foresee in the next?
- What solutions have we tried/have worked/can we forecast for new areas?

### Importance of maintaining standards

As we have already noted on several occasions in these last few chapters, perhaps the biggest benefit for companies introducing competence-based standards and assessment is the potential for *consistency* of performance.

Achieving consistency requires commitment – commitment to effective training and to quality control. All of this requires time and effort on the part of everyone involved.

Most companies have found that the early stages of introduction throw up a range of difficulties, mainly because people are attempting to adjust not only to a new way of working but also to a new way of *thinking*.

Focusing on performance, and on the *outcomes of performance*, requires a shift in thinking. Using new forms of assessment, developing new skills, and taking responsibility for new forms of record keeping all involve a 'learning curve'. Results will not be immediate and no doubt there will be complaints of 'time wasting record keeping' and 'irrelevance' during the first few months.

Early exploratory projects on the accreditation of prior learning demonstrated that even those who were used to assessment (in the more traditional sense) had initial difficulties in operating a competence-based system. However, as assessors and candidates became familiar with the standards, and with their use, the process of assessment became second nature.

The case study from British Gas (see below) provides another perspective on the introduction of NVQs – and another approach. British Gas is using open learning materials, including video, to support the initial training of staff involved in the NVQ programme and is exploring the use of a variety of recording systems. Regional staff have been asked to provide their own estimates of staff time required to operate a competence-based assessment system and the need to link the introduction of this system to a clear organisational culture has been recognised.

Case study

# BRITISH GAS

## Background

British Gas has always adopted a proactive approach to training and development, covering a wide range of employment activities and catering for the provision of basic skills through to high-level professional qualifications. One major area of provision is in technical training, aimed specifically at two craft groups which together form a significant part of the total workforce.

British Gas is an Industry Lead Body and Non-statutory Training Organisation, but is not the sole operator in its field. A large number of engineering contractors and independent gas installers also operate in the UK.

A key attraction of NVQs for the industry is the potentially increased flexibility of training. With a manual workforce of 20,000+ in craft activities, a strong union presence, and the need to cope with a changing environment, the adaptability of the workforce is paramount to successful operation; this adaptability depends in part upon a training system which offers manoeuvrability.

Like many large organisations, British Gas is also a provider of Youth Training Scheme (YTS) places and was therefore quick to identify emerging government directives that competence-standards-based training should be adopted for all national programmes by 1992.

Currently, British Gas is involved in the introduction of two NVQ packages: one for service engineers (NVQ level 3 in customer service) and one for distribution craftsmen (NVQ level 3 in engineering distribution). A submission for NCVQ approval has been prepared in conjunction with City and Guilds. Similar packages have also been submitted to Scotvec, for the eventual award of SVQs in Scotland.

## Assessment

There are 12 British Gas regions – each Region has copies of the defined standards and assessment materials which have been developed centrally. As the new assessment scheme will be 'owned' and used by operational staff, assessors and trainees will all have access to the standards.

Training of primary assessors is to be undertaken through workshops lasting two-and-a-half days. Initial training will be undertaken jointly by trainers and nominated operational staff who will then cascade training to selected operational assessors. The choice of first-line managers as 'registered' assessors was deliberate, to distance the assessor from the assessee. By so doing, assessors are less likely to be influenced by personal factors during the assessment process.

Open learning packages have been developed to support the process of introducing NVQs. These packages include a short video and aim to introduce the standards as well as explain how new NVQs operate. Developed centrally, the open learning packs are to be available to any staff involved in competence-based assessment.

Systems for recording assessment are to be developed and used regionally where City and Guilds external verifiers will operate.

## Verification

British Gas will appoint internal verifiers. Those selected for this role will be from a higher operational level and will operate inter-regionally and within districts. Internal verifiers will have a 'sampling' role within the new scheme. External verifiers from City and Guilds will also operate on a sampling basis.

## Certification

British Gas will pay the City and Guilds certification fees for successful candidates. There are no plans to update existing qualified staff to NVQs, although all staff will attend regular updating training courses, as is usual practice.

## Trades union involvement

Trades unions have been fully informed of plans and progress during development. Terms and conditions of employment have been agreed to reflect the introduction of competence-standards-based training and the flexibility this now provides, together with reference to the acquisition of NVQ and SVQ awards.

## Use of standards

British Gas is considering using the standards for possible job redesign and for structuring training programmes. The latter offers a number of potential improvements and benefits to the organisation. One of the most important, of course, will be the move away from highly structured training, with specific content and time base. A competence-based approach offers British Gas the opportunity to provide better-targeted and more cost-effective training.

## Other NVQs

Working groups have been established to investigate the use of NVQs within other occupational groups. For example, it is expected that the Administrative, Business and Clerical Training Group levels 2 and 3 will be available for staff and clerical categories, although final decisions cannot be made until current reorganisation plans are completed.

British Gas is also involved in the work of the Management Charter Initiative (MCI), concerning both development of management competences and assessment of prior learning. Models of providing access to management qualifications and for achievement of credit for past experience are currently being tested.

## Key issues

One key difficulty is ensuring that the agreed NVQs are generic and accessible to all providers in the industry, including British Gas contractors and independent operators. This has required considerable investment of time at the negotiating table.

The question of systems for recording assessment has yet to be examined in detail. If regionally developed systems are to be used, these must be agreed with the awarding body (ie City and Guilds). One system may, perhaps, emerge as more operationally effective, but a key point is the need to recognise the workload which can be generated by the assessment process.

Each region has provided estimates for annual staff time required for assessment. Line managers' involvement in competence-based assessment is perceived as one component of their responsibility in quality assurance – an estimate of workload allocation is therefore essential to successful implementation. British Gas has recognised that the introduction of competence-based assessment creates a need further to develop an organisational culture in which line managers take ownership for assessment.

There is a clearly identified need to assist operational departments in understanding their role and responsiblities in adopting the competence-based approach. This move from the longstanding traditional methods of training and assessment requires a considerable change in thinking. Assessors (line managers) will not only be given training themselves, but will also require further counselling in order to facilitate this.

A final, but by no means less important, issue concerns health and safety. In an industry in which health and safety directives are of paramount importance, it is important to recognise that first-line assessors may be reluctant to 'sign off competence' based on assessment of individual performance. A formal signature on an assessment document, which states that 'this person is competent in this particular unit of work-based activity' may well have implications for assessors if anything untoward should later occur. To address this, British Gas is actively considering the introduction of certification for assessors. Using the City and Guilds 929 series of qualifications (9292/3/4), British Gas will ensure that all assessors are verified as competent in the assessment role.

These are all issues which must be considered and addressed when introducing NVQs and SVQs. As with many industries, British Gas is clear about the potential benefits, but also aware that lead time is needed to train and develop operational staff and to achieve the required change of attitude.

*Chapter 10*

# Making the Most of the New Standards

## 10.1   Introduction

This chapter looks briefly at ways in which new competence-based standards can be used as a basis for a range of organisational planning and monitoring functions. Rather than presenting an ideal model it raises questions and suggests issues which need to be addressed . Indeed, there can be no ideal model – one of the basic concepts underlying the new forms of competence-based standards is their potential for *flexibility*. To suggest a model for their use would therefore be counter-productive.

If you keep in mind the key points – standards are *outcome-based* and assessment is about collecting *evidence of actual performance* – then you will be able to apply the real potential of competence-based approaches to your own organisational needs.

## 10.2   Standards and organisational development

Implementing a new form of standards which are explicit and measurable gives you the chance to consider and formalise market information and assess how you can capitalise on the opportunities (and minimise constraints) in current and future market scenarios.

Market opportunities in which implementation of standards can probably be most beneficial include:

- need for consistency in quality
- growth in the industry or sector
- introduction of new legislation
- introduction of technological change
- deregulation and competition
- raising of public image of the organisation.

Constraints on the introduction of standards include:

- lack of resources
- complexity and size of the task
- lack of management support
- fragmented sector (which delays standards development anyway).

When planning the evaluation of the introduction of competence-based standards and NVQs in relation to organisation development, the following checklist may be useful:

- What were the key objectives in implementing standards?
- What were the priority objectives?
- What were the objectives in each occupational area?
- What milestones to achievement of objectives have been identified?
- What are the resource implications?
- What actions have had the most impact on acceptance of standards within the company?
- What actions/issues have had the most impact on rejection of standards within the company?

## 10.3    Expanding the use of standards

Once standards are in place for assessment of workplace performance, and for achievement of NVQs, you will be ready to consider their use in other areas of organisational activity.

Your choice of activities, and their priority ordering, will depend very much upon your current organisational structure, and the administrative, managerial and communication systems currently in place.

Standards may be used effectively in the following areas:

- performance appraisal
- manpower planning
- selection and recruitment
- multiskilling
- revision of job descriptions/functions
- training and development.

The last of these is considered in Chapter 12.

Standards can also be updated to incorporate changes within the organisation, including the introduction of new technology or reorganisation.

## 10.4   An action plan

When considering how to expand the use of standards within your organisation, you will need to establish a clear action plan.

Key questions you may consider will include:

- What needs to be done to achieve the introduction of standards for every employee within the organisation?
- Who is going to be responsible for implementation activities?
- In which key areas will we utilise standards (see list above)?
- How long will it take?
- How much will it cost?
- What are our priorities?
- How will we measure progress?

Your action plan may be structured as follows:

- purpose of document
- key objectives, priorities, actions, issues
- personnel resources and management structure
- finances
- standards in use (percentage of workforce)
- standards under development
- timescale
- evaluation
- implementation plan in each area of development.

## 10.5   Standards and performance appraisal

If you are already using standards in continuous assessment of workplace performance (ie within NVQs), the expansion to a performance appraisal system will not be too difficult.

You may treat the ongoing assessment as 'formative' evidence and link this to the annual performance appraisal. There are one or two points to bear in mind in this connection, however.

First, you should avoid making the annual performance appraisal a 'summative' assessment which leads directly to award of NVQs or the units which constitute them. This would encourage a 'time-serving' basis for awards which runs counter to the aims of NVQs – individuals should have access to awards on the basis of their individual performance.

Second, you must consider how such systems will be perceived by those who use them. Assessment for NVQs is directly linked to an incentive/reward system – external recognition through qualification. Performance appraisal is often linked to promotion or merit bonus or salary structure.

You need to be clear how you plan to link the two kinds of assessment. If people achieve NVQs, does this lead automatically to promotion, or salary increase, or merit bonus? What will be the key purpose of the performance appraisal system? Is it a completely 'open' reporting system? Are 'promotion markings' or any part of the report kept secret from the individual? (It is to be hoped that most systems have moved on from this practice.)

When considering the use of competence-based standards in performance appraisal, therefore, you must also consider how your appraisal system links with ongoing assessment of workplace performance and also with any other incentive or reward systems which you currently (or are planning to) operate.

Establishing the performance appraisal system, once your objectives are clear, involves a process of utilising the competence-based standards in a format which will facilitate an annual feedback and review.

If assessment has been continuous throughout the year, then feedback at an appointed annual time should not come as any surprise. The appraisal interview will present a good opportunity for training needs to be clearly identified and agreed, together with a development plan, as well as establishing objectives for the next year. The explicit nature of competence-based standards will provide a sound basis for discussion, as will the requirement for evidence of performance. In short, the nature and purpose of performance appraisal need not change, but the basis for discussion can be more explicit and based on clearer forms of evidence of the past year's performance.

Figure 10.1, taken from Gerald Randell's *Staff Appraisal* (Randell, 19--), may be a helpful guide in considering the *functions* of performance appraisal in your organisation. Once you are clear on the specific functions that are applicable to your existing, or planned scheme, you can consider how best to utilise competence-based standards in this area.

## 10.6   Standards and manpower planning

Manpower planning is the systematic analysis of the company's resources, the construction of a forecast of its future manpower requirements from this base, with special

The purposes of an appraisal scheme are:

– to assess future potential
– to assess training and development needs
– to assess past performance
– to establish control of behaviour
– to bring about changes in behaviour
– to help improve current performance.

The main steps of exercising management control are:

– setting standards
– monitoring performance
– comparing performance with the standard
– taking action that may be needed (either to improve the performance or to change the standards).

The main intentions of an appraisal scheme are:

– *Evaluation*, to enable the organisation to share out money, promotions and perquisites (perks) apparently fairly
– *Auditing*, to discover the work potential, both present and future, of individuals and departments
– *Constructing succession plans* for manpower, departmental and corporate planning
– *Discovering training needs* by exposing inadequacies and deficiencies which could be remedied by training
– *Motivating staff* to reach organisational standards and objectives
– *Developing individuals* by advice, information and attempts at shaping their behaviour by praise or punishment
– *Checking the effectiveness* of personnel procedures and practices.

**Figure 10.1** *The functions of performance appraisal*

Source: Gerald Randell, *Staff Appraisal*, Institute of Personnel Management

concentration on the efficient use of manpower at both these stages, and the planning necessary to ensure that the manpower supply will match the forecast requirement. (Bell, 1974)

Put more simply is: *manpower planning is ensuring that the right number of people are in the right place at the right time.*

When looking forward for your manpower needs, what current measures do you use? How clear are your future plans? How much do you know about the roles that people carry out in your organisation and the actual skills they need; or what new skills will be needed to cope with planned change?

These have always been the difficult questions faced by those responsible for considering the future needs of an organisation. Manpower planning has become a complex and sophisticated activity with computer models and complex mathematical techniques being used in forecasting. Competence-based standards are not going to solve these problems, but because of their explicit nature they can contribute to the more effective identification of skills and knowledge required in new work roles.

Manpower planning is really a series of activities:

- analysis of current resources
- forecasting of future needs
- planning to supply these needs.

The activities of analysing current resources and forecasting future needs relate directly to the performance required. In turn, the performance required relates directly to the skills and knowledge expected of employees.

If performance in monitored on a continuous basis, and the results of this performance measurement collated as part of your evaluation exercise, you will have valuable data to inform your future plans.

## 10.7  Standards, selection and recruitment

This section also incorporates the use of standards in the revision of job descriptions and functions.

Recruitment and selection is about choosing staff. Again this involves a number of activities:

Deciding what $\longrightarrow$ Casting the $\longrightarrow$ Shortlisting $\longrightarrow$ Decision-
the job needs    recruitment                  making
                net

Staff selection may often be a process conducted by gut feeling, despite training of managers and personnel staff in a wide range of techniques. The use of clearly defined standards can help to develop this gut feeling approach into a more informed and informative one, for both the interviewer and the interviewee.

Let's take the first activity – deciding *what the job needs*.

If competence-based standards have been introduced, then the expectations of the job someone undertakes will be clearly defined in terms of standards or expectations of performance. These standards will include the skills and knowledge required, and a specified range of activities in which performance must be undertaken.

This then, will provide the basis on which a job specification and person specification can be devised.

In *casting the recruitment net* you may wish to consider which competence-based qualifications would provide evidence of the performance level you are seeking. In particular, there may be specific units of competence which make up the specification you have developed.

You can consider whether you need someone who has attained all the relevant units, or whether you are prepared to take someone who has *some* of them, requiring you to arrange training in those remaining.

This consideration of NVQs held by prospective candidates may be a consideration more for the future – NVQs are as yet fairly new and it will take some time for their full use in the labour market to be established. However, the exercise of planning by units of competence does help to focus your mind, and the minds of the prospective employees, on the issue of evidence of performance. This approach will contribute to your shortlisting and decision-making exercises. What evidence can candidates supply of their current level of expertise? How valid is that evidence?

You may even want to consider establishing an initial assessment for interviewees, or asking them to present what they feel is valid evidence of their current level of performance.

Don't forget also that the National Record of Vocational Achievement (NROVA see p 70) is in itself a type of portfolio of evidence. Some certificates contained within it may be more of the traditional type, and some (especially for young people) may have been obtained on particular work experience or national training programmes, but it is a useful source of information.

## 10.8   Standards and multiskilling

Because the process of 'multiskilling' involves looking at the transferability of skills and the relationship between various activities within an organisational structure, competence-based standards are of particular help in this area.

You will recall from Part I that competence-based standards are derived through a process of *functional* analysis. A focus on functions rather than tasks contributes to a broader view of competence and incorporates aspects of task and contingency management as well as operating within the working environment.

This functional basis of standards can be used to facilitate your analysis and planning of multiskilling activities. Industry Lead Bodies may even be able to supply you with details of the original functional analysis which led to the derivation of competence-based standards. Alternatively, a good external consultant who has worked on competence-based developments will be able to assist you.

An overview of the sectoral standards, particularly at the higher levels of 'key work roles' (from which units of competence are derived) will also give you valuable information.

## Chapter 11

# Making the Most of New Forms of Assessment

Within the new system of NVQs, assessment is 'a process of obtaining evidence and making judgements about that evidence' (Technical Advisory Group 1989). More traditional forms of assessment require assessors both to determine the standards to be achieved and to assess evidence against those standards (as in a course-based programme of study). Within NVQs, the standards are already established and are in explicit (and written) format for both assessor and assessee. Assessment decisions therefore focus on whether the assessee has presented sufficient evidence of the right quality.

## 11.1 Evidence of competence

Assessment of normal work performance offers the most natural form of evidence of competence. Where this is not possible, perhaps due to operational constraints or requirements of health and safety, workplace assessment can be supplemented by simulations, or by competency tests (like skills tests). In general, most observation of workplace assessment will need to be supplemented by at least oral questioning in order to determine evidence of transferability of skills and knowledge application across the specified range of work activity.

Evidence of performance can also be obtained during the course of a training programme when trainees practise and demonstrate skills and application of knowledge. In this way, assessment can be integrated with the learning process and provide useful feedback to trainees.

Given this performance-focused nature of new forms of assessment, how best can they be used to benefit your company?

## 11.2 Performance appraisal and manpower planning

The previous chapter briefly outlined the use of competence-based standards within performance appraisal systems, and suggested that ongoing assessment may be treated as formative and thus contribute to the annual performance appraisal. It is worth noting again here, though, that you should avoid making the annual performance appraisal a 'summative' assessment which leads directly to the award of an NVQ. This would reinstate a time-based element to the achievement of NVQs, whereas one of their key benefits is individual access to awards based on individual performance.

Ongoing assessment, using competence-based systems, provides an up-to-date audit of individual and group performance. You might want to consider the best ways in which you can collate information to maintain your own records of improved performance.

As individuals are assessed, and achieve units of competence, you may wish to record this centrally to contribute to your manpower planning activities. This is also particularly relevant where you need to draw together project teams for particular assignments. You might consider the use of computerised systems for recording current skill levels; there are a variety available or under development which can be used for this purpose.

## 11.3 Assessment and training

The design and delivery of training, using competence-based

standards and assessment, is perhaps one of the most attractive benefits to individual companies. For this reason, Chapter 12 deals exclusively with this issue.

However, the issue of assessment in relation to training needs analysis and evaluation is also a key contributor to improvement of company performance.

## 11.4   Training needs analysis

Using explicit standards of performance, assessment of current levels of skill and knowledge, and identification of the 'training gap' are greatly facilitated. This process also ensures a common standard both for the initial assessment process, and for the targeted training which follows.

Trainers will need to be experienced in the use of competence-based standards and in their assessment. Line managers, if trained in work-based assessment, will be in an ideal position to identify training needs of both individuals and groups and pass this information on to the training department.

This somewhat changes the role of the trainer, but in line with current trends. The trainer becomes a key adviser and consultant in the company and provides support to line managers in both the needs-analysis and solution-finding role.

## 11.5   Accreditation of prior learning (APL)

Earlier chapters briefly outlined the APL concept and process. However, it is in the context of training needs analysis that APL becomes a truly valuable tool.

It is worth reiterating that APL is not an autonomous process, but an integral part of competence-based assessment. When operated in-company, or within an 'approved' assessment centre (see below), it requires trained assessors, and may involve additional verification costs. However, it is likely that the return on what is usually a minor investment in these areas will be well worth the commitment.

'APL is a process which enables the identification, assessment and certification of a person's vocationally relevant past achievements' (BTEC, 1990). One of the key purposes of APL at national level is to improve *access* to vocational qualifications. Many adults, for example, are reluctant to return to long periods of study in order to obtain a qualification when they feel they would simply be repeating learning in order to prove that they can do what they already do every day!

On an organisational (ie company) level, APL can offer a solution to this adult perception and be used as a motivational tool to encourage individual and group development. In addition, the company benefits by improved targeting of training – to say nothing of a more cost-effective use of the training budget.

We might think of APL as a kind of skills audit or training audit. It can also be an initial motivator for the introduction of competence-based standards and NVQs, offering credit towards NVQs for those who can successfully provide evidence of competence which matches the specified standards.

All the major awarding bodies now have policies and published guidelines regarding APL, and verification processes are being included across many occupational sectors.

If you are considering using APL, first review the hypothetical scenario which follows, then contact the relevant awarding bodies for the NVQs you plan to use to check that APL guidelines are in place.

The purpose of APL guidelines in each occupational area are twofold. First, they help assessors with information on the types of evidence which will be acceptable; and second, they provide help for external (ie awarding body) verifiers.

Let's consider a hypothetical scenario for introducing APL.

## Company X introducing APL

Company X, which operates in the manufacturing sector, employs 5,000 people on a national basis. Occupations include those in the manufacturing process, administrative and management staff.

Relevant standards and NVQs have been identified and plans for their introduction are under consideration.

The company would like to use the competence-based assessment process to take a skills audit of its workforce and appreciates that the use of APL would facilitate this, providing a motivator for staff, and being an integral part of the planned change.

It explores the possibility of using APL with relevant awarding bodies and finds that policies and guidelines are in place. The requirements of operating APL include:

- assessors who are trained in the concepts and operation of APL
- verification arrangements agreed with awarding body.

The company had planned to train line managers and trainers in work-based assessment and explored the use of external consultants to undertake this work. They checked that the consultants were fully capable of delivering a training package which included APL concepts and techniques. They also checked that the consultants were approved by the appropriate awarding bodies. This enabled the company to link training and verification of assessors to award of qualifications in assessment, thus providing a further motivator for staff who had been designated to the assessment role.

Discussions with the awarding body regarding verification arrangements revealed that arrangements for external verifiers to visit the company could be negotiated on the basis of the number of assessors and candidates. A verifier would monitor the work of a number of assessors. The company would be required to pay a daily rate for each verification visit.

The company then considered its internal policy and operational arrangements and set up a management group to establish:

- a company policy on APL

- a named individual with overall responsibility for the introduction and operation of APL in-company
- a staff development programme.

The decision to pilot APL with the administrative staff in one region was taken. Appropriate staff were designated as assessors and were trained in both work-based assessment and APL, using published competence-based standards as the basis for assessment.

Administrative staff were provided with details of the pilot through an article in the company newsletter. Line managers were briefed at regular network meetings and then discussed the pilot with their staff during regular staff meetings. Volunteers were sought and identified.

Those staff selected for the pilot met with their designated assessor to draw up an assessment plan. This identified the units of competence for which individual staff felt they could provide sufficient evidence of current performance. A timescale for assessment was also agreed.

Individual staff had been made fully aware that the collection of evidence from past achievements was entirely their responsibility, as was the organisation of this evidence into a 'portfolio'. Each individual had a copy of the relevant standards of performance and would organise their portfolio to match the specified units and elements of competence.

The company allowed individuals time for the collection of evidence, arranged on an individual basis with line managers. Designated assessors (who were also line managers in some instances) provided ongoing support and advice during the evidence-collection stage.

All designated assessors met on a regular basis to exchange ideas regarding progress and to provide a forum for assessor support. The APL manager (who had been established at policy-making level and had overall responsibility for the introduction and operation of APL) attended assessor meetings and also visited individual candidates to monitor and report on general progress.

When individual candidates had completed their portfolio, with guidance and support from their designated assessor, the assessor conducted a final review of evidence presented. If satisfied with the *validity*, *currency*, *authenticity* and *sufficiency* of the evidence, the assessor then made a recommendation for award of appropriate units.

The evidence was reviewed by an external verifier who either decided to support the claim for credit, or referred any discrepancies back to the assessor. The individual concerned was informed of any difficulties and given the opportunity to provide further evidence for reassessment.

Successful individuals were awarded the units for which sufficient and valid evidence had been presented. The awarding body issued 'credit notes' for each unit which could be retained by the individual. The company paid for the issue of these unit certificates at £6 per unit.

A final review of achievements led to mutual agreement of training needs and future development plans. These were recorded on the individual development plan and reported to the training department. The individual's training needs would therefore be recorded and appropriate training solutions planned.

## 11.6  Individual development plans

The introduction and use of individual development plans are worth consideration. As competence-based assessment is *individualised*, linking assessment to personal and career development becomes a simpler process to operate within the company.

Again, you will need to consider the supporting structure of development plans and career progression. You may need to modify your existing in-company schemes, particularly in the context of documentation and recording systems. You might also like to consider ways in which *self-assessment* can be incorporated into the ongoing development process.

Information from individual development plans could be collated to contribute to annual training strategies and detailed plans.

## 11.7 Meeting NVQ criteria

Whether you use documentation and procedures available within the relevant NVQ structure, or you choose to devise your own, a key requirement is that the assessment scheme meets the criteria set by the NCVQ. These criteria are summarised in Part III.

The NVQ criteria relate to *quality of assessment* and *maintenance of national standards*. They also ensure that an *equal opportunities policy* is incorporated into working practice.

If you operate an in-company assessment scheme, you may want to link the development of your employees to in-company training programmes. This is acceptable as long as your in-company specifications for achievement of NVQs does not make completion of these training programmes mandatory.

Individuals may learn in a variety of ways, including through work experience. NVQs are awarded for *successful assessment of competence performance*, not for attendance on specified courses.

## 11.8 Getting help

If you are considering ways in which you can make the best use of competence-based assessment, there are a number of sources of information and direct support.

### Awarding bodies

These bodies will be able to provide information regarding assessment requirements for particular NVQs, and for APL. They also provide external verifiers and can advise you of the fees involved. Remember, some Industry Lead Bodies are also awarding bodies.

## Colleges

Many colleges have now radically changed their provision and some operate as approved assessment centres. Check with your local college provider to see what services are available. These may include college assessors who can visit the company, APL, or assistance with development programmes. Make sure the college has trained assessors and the facilities to assess in relevant occupational areas.

## Private providers

Some private training providers will be recommended by Industry Lead Bodies and awarding bodies and can help you with the development of standards, introduction of competence-based assessment, APL, assessor training and so on. Make sure you choose a provider who has experience in the field of competence-based provision.

## Accredited Training Centres

The majority of these centres, which offer training in relation to national training programmes (eg YTS and ET) are based in colleges. Their provision has recently expanded to include a more diverse range of training programmes. They can also assist with assessor training.

Whichever type of assistance you choose, it is best first to consider exactly what type of help you need within all areas of competence-based provision. It is usually advantageous to use a single source which can provide help across the board than to find you have to contract with two or three different organisations to achieve your total objectives.

Case study

# COVENTRY TECHNICAL COLLEGE – A COLLEGE/INDUSTRY COLLABORATION

Coventry Technical College has been involved for some time in national projects which have explored the use of competence-based provision. The College is currently working with a large company to establish a model of collaborative work on this issue.

Through its contact with local employers, the College has recognised the increasing awareness of the need to invest in human resource as well as to enhance flexibility and transfer of skills. It has explored the use of records of achievement which can be used to document the abilities of an individual and can also serve as a vehicle for accumulating nationally recognised credits for competence. A key issue, the College believes, is ensuring that the myriad records of achievement and personal portfolios being produced by schools, companies and further and higher education establishments are compatible both with each other and with the NCVQ's National Record of Vocational Achievement (NROVA).

A common goal in all developments is to record performance against target. Coventry Technical College therefore believes that the issues and difficulties associated with implementing competence-based systems and processes are concerned with making decisions about the nature of targets. Who sets them and can they be altered? How do we measure performance? Who does this and where?

## Working with local companies

Working in partnership with companies, Coventry Technical College would first help to devise a competence map of the employment positions in the company. With job descriptions effectively translated into elements of competence, it is then possible to identify the ability of the employees to do a job. Further, it serves as a career map and training action plan by indicating the competences required by an individual in order to seek transfer and promotion to another job. Importantly, the format and language used to prescribe the competence map must be similar to or compatible with that of the performance targets specified for nationally recognised qualifications.

With this facilitity the company can enable and entitle employees to be assessed and be given credit for their achievement as measured against the targets which are the competence requirements for the job.

Some companies might want to give their own mark of accreditation and enable their employees to develop personal portfolios.

What is of greater value for the employee – and consequently the employer – is for the individual's achievement to be given national accreditation and the portfolio used as a vehicle for the accumulation of credit towards a nationally recognised qualification.

Hence, Coventry Technical College sees its role (and that of FE colleges generally) in forging partnerships with companies to assist in the design of competence maps with a format and language structure compatible with the performance targets of nationally recognised qualifications.

College tutors can be used to assess the competence of company employees directly or to audit the assessment practice of workplace supervisors. The latter practice is possible since the commonly agreed performance targets clearly specify the assessment criteria to be used. The College–industry partnership can then negotiate the new learning requirements of the individual concerned and devise a suitable experience including study in College, in the workplace and at home. The role of the College tutor is to ensure that any new managed learning experience leads to achievement which can claim units of credit towards nationally recognised qualifications.

The approved NVQs provide an immediately useful means of gaining qualifications by credit accumulation. Meanwhile, many other nationally recognised qualifications can be delivered in modular format and gained through unit credit accumulation following study in College and the workplace. BTEC certificates, diplomas and continuing education certificates are such examples.

## Proposed action plan – College–industry partnership

1. *Company competence map*
Devised by employees, supervisors and college tutors acting as consultants
2. *Individual competence file*
Initial assessment of competence by company personnel, supervisors, college assessors (at cost)
3. *Individual action plan*
Design of new learning programme required to meet needs of external certification by employee, supervisor, and college tutor.

The most cost-effective way to meet this objective at present is for companies to provide personnel/counselling services to their employees to enable the identification of current levels of competence and

162

qualifications required. The candidate is then referred to the college of further education.

At Coventry Technical College, 'quality of product' is equivalent to 'successful students'. The process by which the college 'manufactures' its products is illustrated in Figure 11.1

## COVENTRY TECHNICAL COLLEGE

## ACCREDITATION OF PRIOR LEARNING AND ACHIEVEMENT

Coventry Technical college is committed to the extension and development of the Accreditation of Prior Learning and Achievement, as part of the wider objectives of increasing flexibility, access and participation and of establishing a mechanism for a shorter route to a qualification.

### APL/APA - Definition

The view is taken within the College that APA is one of many forms of assessment. Assessment is seen to be the process of making judgements about the validity, sufficiency, authenticity and recency of evidence offered as proof of competence. Forms of evidence alternative to the nature of evidence collected in direct assessment situations may be offered in support of claims of competence acquired in the past. This evidence may need to be supported by current evidence produced at the assessment centre at the request of the assessor in charge.

### The Student Portfolio

The development of a document known as the STUDENT PORTFOLIO has been the central focus for developments. The structure and format of the Student Portfolio rationalises the process of administration of applications, enrolment, course design, learning, assessment and the final award of a qualification. It is a document which is developed and owned by the student. It is the central location for his or her personal data and documentation, and

# THE C. T. C. CURRICULUM

## Process of Manufacture

* *carry out initial guidance and counselling to analyse training needs*

* *assess and give credit for current level of competence*

* *deliver new learning and assessment programme, on and off-site at a pace which suits the individual*

* *'bridge the gap' and bring to qualified status*

* *negotiate progress and record achievement*

* *ensure student (product) is aware of own capabilities and able to do a job of work*

Figure 11.1 *The 'manufacturing process'.* Coventry Technical College

is the vehicle for recording achievement and accumulating credit towards a qualification.

The Student Portfolio contains:

(i) **Guidance Notes** which explain the support system available and the opportunity to gain credit for prior achievement.

An initial action plan is developed as the student chooses an appropriate qualification route.

(ii) **Programme and Module Descriptors** which specify the performance targets or achievements required for success in gaining the qualification/

This information is required by counsellors and students when choosing an appropriate qualification and collecting evidence for assessment of prior learning.

(iii) **Records of Achievement** which record the student's achievement or assessed level of performance against the set targets. The Record of Achievement includes:-

Statement of Curricular Achievement
Student Summary Statement
Externally Awarded Qualifications
Curriculum Vitae (Optional)

Students begin to develop their Portfolio at the point of application. Using the standard documents designed by the project teams the student with the help of counsellors and tutors can match their previous achievements against those required for success in a module and may be accredited.

Current and Future Developments

Over the last two years there has been an increase in the numbers of mature students claiming accreditation for prior achievements. The extension of the process now includes post-16 students and in principle the process has involved all full-time courses from September 1990 in line with the student curriculum entitlement through TVEI extension. The project focus has, however, concentrated on seven courses from September 1990 (approximately 96 students), where progress is being monitored in greater detail. The information gained is to be used to benefit a wider range of course provision, with the explicit intention of widespread extension within the college by 1992.

## Chapter 12

# Competence-based Training

As we noted in earlier chapters, the flexibility provided by competence-based systems is one of the key attractions for employers. With explicit standards of performance to use as a base, and tools such as accreditation of prior learning (APL) to both facilitate training needs analysis and motivate employees, the attraction is clear.

However, if training is to be effective, both in terms of improving performance and in relation to costs, then trainers must understand the key concepts and issues involved in the development of competence-based standards.

Trainers with responsibility for the design of programmes need to understand how standards are developed. This is outlined briefly in Part I, but a synopsis of development methodology is given here as a reference point.

## 12.1 Standards development

Competence-based standards are *employment-led*. This means they are developed *by* the industry, *for* the industry. They therefore reflect the expectations of employment.

Standards are developed at *sector level* and through a process of *functional analysis*. This involves beginning with the *key purpose* of the sectoral occupation and identifying the *key functions* undertaken.

The concept of functions is highly important. Many earlier analysis techniques focused on tasks, which represent a lower level of activity. The following may be helpful in distinguishing between these different terms:

Tasks – activities undertaken at work
Functions – the purpose of activities undertaken at work.

This is a very broad-brush distinction, but it recognises the need to identify *outcomes* of activity when deriving occupational standards of competence. By asking why an activity is undertaken, one is establishing the purpose of the activity, which leads to the outcome or result of that activity.

Identifying outcomes maintains a focus on *performance*. Competence-based standards, as noted above, must reflect expectations of workplace performance.

Once the outcomes have been identified, and established as either *units of competence* or as *elements of competence* (see below), the next question is 'What are the qualities of these outcomes that indicate competent performance?'

The terms *units* and *elements of competence* were explained in Part I (Chapter 3). As a brief reminder, a *unit of competence* represents work activity which:

- can be undertaken by one individual
- is worthy of separate certification (ie as a 'credit' towards a full NVQ).

An *element of competence* is:

- a description of something which a person who works in a given occupational area should be able to do. It reflects action, behaviour or outcomes which have real meaning in the occupational sector to which it relates.

When we ask 'what are the qualities of these outcomes', therefore, we are seeking the *criteria* by which an assessor can judge whether an individual's performance meets the required standard. The results of our research into qualities therefore, provide us with *performance criteria*. These reflect the critical aspects of performance – all those qualities which are essential to competent performance.

A final stage of deriving standards refers to the range of contexts, conditions or contingencies in which a competent person must operate. These are researched and incorporated into a *range statement*.

Some standards defined by Industry Lead Bodies may also include statements relating to *evidence*. This is a guideline for assessors providing information on the type or range of evidence – both performance evidence and knowledge evidence – required.

One question often asked is 'If competence-based standards focus on performance what about the *knowledge* that people need to do their job competently?' A basic concept underlying the development of competence-based standards is that application of knowledge is an integrated part of competent performance. This means two things:

- it is application of knowledge and not knowledge itself that is important to competent performance
- application of knowledge can be assessed through assessment of competence performance.

*Some* knowledge will be *implicit* in assessment of performance. For example, if an individual performs competently (ie to specified standards) on a similar activity, but in a different context, then an assessor may, with reasonable safety, assume that that individual has successfully applied knowledge of similar, but not identical, working requirements to the second situation.

In some situations, assessors may need to collect evidence of relevant application of knowledge through *oral questioning*.

It may not be possible to observe an individual performing in the complete range of workplace activities, or to assess the full amount of knowledge required, simply by observation of performance. In this instance, other forms of assessment may be used. These may include simulation, oral questioning, skills test or assignment.

Readers can supplement this very brief outline of standards development methodology by reading Part I. Further technical information can be found in the documents provided by the Training Agency (now TEED) (which are listed in the Reference Section of Part III).

## 12.2  Standards, NVQs and training programmes

One important point, made several times in Part I, is that NVQs have *nothing whatsoever to do with training programmes*. This addresses the common misconception that units of competence are training modules. This is far from correct.

A unit of competence is a unit of *assessment* and *certification*. The standards (elements, performance criteria and range statements) incorporated within a unit of competence, specify the *performance* required in the workplace.

Units of competence are *outcome-based*
Training modules are *input-based*.

Training modules are designed to provide the development (or input) that individuals and groups need in order to achieve and maintain the required standards. They may contain practical exercises and assignments, but these represent practice rather than actual performance in the main.

Assessment of practical work on a training programme should be to the same standards as those used in the workplace. Evidence of performance in these practical exercises can *contribute towards* final achievement of the relevant unit, but should not serve as a 'one-off' or any form of 'single judgement'.

The issue of *standards development* and the distinction between *units of competence* and *training modules* is critical to succesful training design. You should make sure you are clear on these issues if you are planning the design of competence-based training.

## 12.3   Designing competence-based training

Experience with a wide range of trainers indicates that the key difficulty they experience in the design of competence-based training is the switch in thinking required to think in *outcome* terms.

Any trainer experienced in the design of training programmes automatically thinks in terms of training objectives and content. Competence-based training still has objectives and still has a clear content. The essential difference is that explicit, *outcome-based* standards are used as the basis of design.

Once trainers have grasped the concepts involved, the actual task of design is far less daunting. As with all competence-based activities, the design starts with standards.

The trainer should review the standards relevant to the work role of the target audience and ask the following questions:

- What do people actually have to *do*?
- What underpinning knowledge and skill do they need?
- What training activities would best suit
  - the target audience?
  - the contribution of training to achievement of standards?
  - the constraints of time, cost, location?
- What assessment activities can be built in to the training programme?
- How can the training be evaluated?

You will notice that these questions are not too far removed from current practice. Standards, and the components of standards, are more explicit, facilitating the use of assessment activities within the training programme, and thus providing ideal opportunities for self-, peer and trainer assessment.

If trainers focus on the key concepts outlined above and on the key questions to be applied to the design of training, they will have made a good start on introducing competence-based training within the company.

## 12.4 Training evaluation

If you build assessment activities into your training programmes, you are already contributing to an effective evaluation of the training itself, as well as providing motivation and feedback for your participants.

You should also plan a longer-term evaluation in advance, again using competence-based standards as a foundation for this planning.

As the standards specify both what individuals must do and how well they must do it (in the workplace), the standards themselves provide the *workplace performance measures*.

To conduct a realistic evaluation of training effectiveness, you will first need to take a measure of current performance. If your company has introduced accreditation of prior learning (see p 154), information on this initial measurement of current performance will be available. If not, you might consider ways in which you can collect it.

If you are familiar with the concept of evidence of competence – particularly if you have been trained in workplace assessment – you will be able to plan this initial measuring of performance as a process of evidence collection. The nature and type of evidence will depend on the context, the operational requirements and the time constraints involved.

A brief measurement of current performance could be established through a pre-course questionnaire, or pre-course exercise. This would give you a starting point, but would obviously not be as effective as a more detailed assessment. Pre-course documentation should be provided to both target audience and their line managers. If you obtain an assessment (independently) from both, you will be able to make some comparison of results.

Your pre-course documentation should be carefully planned, and should include the specific standards used in designing the training programme.

Post-course evaluation then follows a similar pattern. The key purpose of training is to improve performance; your evaluation should therefore aim to identify clear improvement in performance.

If you have close liaison with the section heads and line managers, you could set up a short-term assessment system to contribute to your evaluation exercise. However, if your company has introduced NVQs, line managers should be assessing competence on a regular basis, and recording the results (evidence) of assessment – so you will have a ready-made assessment system. If your company has also introduced individual development plans (see p 158), then most of your work has been done already!

## 12.5   Using external providers

If you don't design your own in-company training, or if you use external providers for some training design and delivery, the same rules apply. However, as has been mentioned several times already, make sure you choose a provider who has experience in competence-based developments, and particularly one who understands the concepts and issues involved.

## 12.6   Gaining external recognition for in-company training

Another question often asked, and which illustrates yet another misconception about new competence-based developments, is

'How can we get our training accredited by the NCVQ? If you have grasped the key concepts outlined within this book, you will know that the answer to this is that you can't.

The NCVQ does not accredit training programmes. NVQs are comprised of units of assessment and can only be achieved by successful *assessment of workplace performance.*

Should your company wish to gain recognition for its in-company training, however, this can be achieved. The recognition of training usually takes one of two forms: credit exemption and advanced standing.

Credit exemption and advanced standing can be negotiated with educational institutions. A formal agreement (with a provider of a specific programme of study) is established. This allows individuals to be 'exempt from' or to be 'credited with' certain parts of that programme. It is the relationship to a specific programme of study which distinguishes this form of credit from that involved in the APL process. NVQs are not linked to any one programme of study. Units within an NVQ are units of assessment (not training units). Awards of NVQs therefore denotes workplace performance achievement not learning achievement.

With NVQs:

- assessment of performance (competence-based) is individualised
- assessment of performance (competence-based) can lead to award of national vocational qualifications.

External recognition of (in-company) training programmes refers to (approval of) the actual content, duration, delivery etc of the learning programme itself. Anyone who completes the (approved) learning programme can gain 'credit exemption' or 'advanced standing' for a specified course of study.

One of the most widely known systems of this type is the CATS scheme (credit accumulation and transfer). This is operated by the CNAA (Council for National Academic Awards) and offers a system whereby credits obtained through approved learning programmes can be counted towards a first degree – even if those credits were obtained in different places and at different times.

This system of 'credit rating' is useful if your workforce usually aim for degrees or professional qualifications – but you should remember that higher-level qualifications are also being revised to a competence-based format.

The developments undertaken by the Management Charter Initiative (MCI) under the direction of the National Forum for Management Education and Development (NFMED) have created much interest, particularly in the last year as draft competences for managers have emerged.

The following, and final case study provides information on MCI's Experienced Manager APL Project and offers valuable information for all companies considering the introduction of the accreditation of prior learning (APL) process and/or the use of management competences.

Case study

# ACCREDITATION OF PRIOR LEARNING FOR EXPERIENCED MANAGERS

The Management Charter Initiative (MCI), the Industry Lead Body for development of national standards of competence for managers, embarked on a major APL pilot project in September 1989, funded by the Training Agency. The project seeks to:

- develop a credible and rigorous APL methodology for experienced managers
- pilot-test it with academic and non-academic centres including employers
- develop a national implementation strategy.

The proposal for the project came from the Experienced Managers Working Party, set up under the chairmanship of Paul Jervis of the

Bristol Business School. This working party, established in late 1988 to address the development needs of experienced managers, reports into the Standards Development Committee of the National Forum for Management Education and Development, MCI's parent body.

There are now 13 pilot centres participating, ranging from training providers and colleges in England and Scotland to MCI networks and employers. British Rail, British Gas and the British Institute of Management are all directly involved. All centres have sought accreditation from either BTEC, SCOTVEC or the CNAA for certificate qualifications (the MCI is currently working with these and other awarding bodies to develop NVQs and SVQs based on its national competence standards).

## How does APL work?

APL focuses directly on the national standards of management competence developed by the MCI. These are incorporated into a workbook designed specifically for managers.

APL involves managers reflecting on their own experience, analysing competences gained against units of national standards and developing a portfolio of evidence to demonstrate that competence. Each unit represents a credit towards a qualification, ultimately an NVQ in management.

The kinds of evidence managers are bringing forward include minutes and action points of meetings, letters and memos, business plans, appraisal forms and certificates of training. In addition, managers support their evidence with their own personal accounts of performance, reflecting on what they did and why.

Figure 12.1 shows how the MCI's model works.

Group work is a particular feature of the process. Managers attend workshops and in most centres form peer groups to review experience and evidence.

In each centre, there are trained assessors as well as APL advisors who guide managers through the process.

The project is due to end in April 1991. Evaluation is taking place in the first quarter of 1991. However, initial findings are as shown below.

### There is much enthusiasm for APL among participants

Perhaps the most important and encouraging finding is that the APL process works. Candidates have been able to produce portfolios that can be used to assess their competence. Participants in the process are

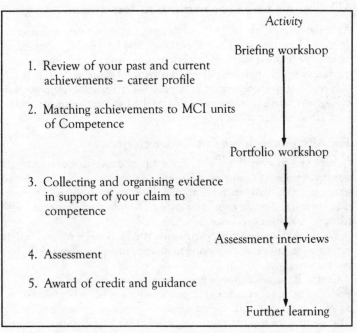

**Figure 12.1** *The MCI model of APL*

enthusiastic about their involvement with APL. There is clear evidence that APL will be a popular route with experienced managers.

## APL is a broader process than we originally thought

In the context of our original definition of the problem of experienced managers, APL was seen as a useful tool that would be used within some form of management development activity.

It was envisaged that APL (or some other technique) would be used to identify where experienced managers were competent (and thus where they were not) as a precursor to a development activity aimed at filling the competence gaps so identified.

Experience to date indicates that this model underestimates the value of the APL process itself as a vehicle for personal development. We now believe that there is considerable developmental value in the APL process itself (at least as it has been designed and operated in the project).

### APL does not have to be restricted to "experienced managers"

Although the work on APL of managerial competence has been developed in the context of a working party looking at the management development needs of 'experienced managers' as defined above, we can now see that the process can be used more widely. It is not only relevant to 'experienced managers' – it is a portfolio approach to management development and could be used as the assessment vehicle for a structured learning programme.

### The APL process is not suitable for everybody

Perhaps as a counter to the above, there is evidence that not everyone is suited to the APL process. The reasons why some find more problems with APL than others seem more likely to lie in issues of personality, personal characteristics and style than in factors connected with education, work experience or job.

We think it is important, particularly if APL is to be offered widely in future, that more work is done to identify those for whom APL may be less successful.

One indication to emerge from our work so far is that, since APL is a self-managed process, it needs people who are self-reliant. It may be possible to identify other characteristics necessary to cope with the APL process, or to indicate in more detail the support structure that might be necessary to prevent problems arising.

### APL is not easy, nor is it cheap, and there can be a high drop-out rate

An indicator of the demanding nature of APL is that there can be a high drop-out rate. Our experience shows that it is very important to get participants' expectations right at the outset. They must not expect the process to be 'quick and dirty' and they must recognise the need, and be prepared, to put in a considerable amount of effort themselves.

We noted with interest that the pilot centres charging the most for the APL process had the lowest drop-out rates. In part, this is to be expected. If people are paying large sums of money, they are likely to persist to ensure that they do get value from their investment. But this may also indicate that the centres concerned have managed, by making the process appear expensive, to indicate to participants at the outset the scale of the commitment they need to make.

Another factor that may influence drop-out rates is the degree of support participants received from the centres at which they are registered. The evaluation of the project when finished will need to investigate whether there are any clear links between completion rates and levels of support provided.

At this stage, it is difficult to put a cost on the typical APL process for experienced managers. However, it is becoming clear that APL is *not* a low-cost way of obtaining management qualifications. It is likely that when detailed cost estimates are available, APL will be seen as an effective and high-quality way of proving managerial competence rather than a cheap alternative to conventional 'training'.

### APL is not easy for the unwaged

Initial indications are that APL, when related to management competences, is not easy for those not currently in employment. The main reason for this, appears to be the accessibility of 'evidence' needed to demonstrate competence. Even if participants have reached the required level of competence in former employment, if they are no longer with the relevant employers they can face difficulties in collecting a sufficient portfolio of evidence.

### The 'ownership' of the APL process is a key factor

The pilot projects have included those based on employers, on polytechnics and colleges, on management development and training organisations, and on professional bodies. This will enable the evaluation to determine whether any one form of organisation and management of the APL process is better than any other.

Preliminary indications are that the employer-based models may offer a number of advantages. However, if this does prove to be true, it will raise other questions about the best form of partnership between employers and training providers.

### MCI APL centres

From early 1991, the MCI will be seeking new centres, including its own networks, to deliver APL under the MCI's name. The MCI will take on the central promotional role, keeping a register of centres and trained assessors and providing marketing facilities. The MCI will also be offering APL directly to employers.

The APL product will consist of:

- workbook for experienced managers
- guidelines for APL assessors
- guidelines for APL advisors
- manual for APL centres
- training for APL assessors and advisors.

(Further information can be gained from the APL Project Director, Jackie Hall, at the MCI on 071-257 4193.)

## 12.7 Summary

This book has attempted to combine an understanding of key concepts with a practical application of new developments in competence-based provision.

I trust that the text, together with its checklists and the various perspectives provided by the case studies have served to give you a clearer insight into these developments, helped you to avoid some of the pitfalls, and provided you with some tools for active decision-making and hands-on experience.

In Part III, you will find references, addresses and other useful material which will be useful as a resource for helping you through your company's change programme.

# PART III
# Help Menu:
# Information,
# Addresses and
# References
# for Practitioners

# Quick Reference Guide

# National Vocational Qualifications - Criteria for Accreditation*

This chapter sets out the criteria used by the NCVQ to decide whether or not a qualification can be accepted as part of the national framework of vocational qualifications.

The criteria are stated without detailed explanation or examples; those interested in submitting qualifications for accreditation should consult the more detailed publication *A Guide to Accreditation*.

## Fundamental criteria

To be accredited as a National Vocational Qualification, a qualification must be:

- based firmly on national standards required for performance in employment, and take proper account of future needs with particular regard to technology, markets and employment patterns;
- based on assessment of the outcomes of learning, specified independently of any particular mode, duration or location of learning;

* Reproduced by kind permission of the NCVQ.

- awarded on the basis of valid and reliable assessments made in such a way as to ensure that performance to the national standard can be achieved at work;
- free from barriers which restrict access and progression, and available to all those who are able to reach the required standard by whatever means;
- free from overt or covert discriminatory practices with regard to gender, age, race or creed and designed to pay due regard to the special needs of individuals.

# 1  Statements of competence

1.1 All NVQs must consist of an agreed **statement of competence**, which should be determined or endorsed by a **Lead Body** with responsibility for defining, maintaining and improving national standards of performance in the sectors of employment where the competence is practised.

1.2 Responsibility for defining standards of competence rests with the recognised Lead Body, which should involve the appropriate employer, employee, professional , educational and training interests across the United Kingdom.

1.3 Competence must be specified in an NVQ statement of competence in a way which provides for **breadth** of application, so that:

1.3.1 the area of competence covered has meaning and relevance in the sector or employment concerned;

1.3.2 the competence covered is broadly comparable with other NVQs at the same level, particularly those in similar or adjacent areas;

1.3.3 the range of competence is broad enough to give flexibility in employment and enhance employment opportunities;

1.3.4 a basis for progression in both the sector concerned and related sectors is provided;

1.3.5 adaptation to meet new and emering occupational patterns is facilitated;

1.3.6 there is no overt or covert discrimination against any section of the community in the wording or content of the statement of competence;

1.3.7 the statement of competence is informed by relevant European developments on the comparability of qualifications.

1.4 The NVQ statement of competence should be derived from an analysis of functions within the area of competence to which it relates. It should reflect:

1.4.1 competence relating to task management, safety and the ability to deal with organisational environments, relationships with other people and unexpected events;

1.4.2 the ability to transfer the competence from place to place and context to context;

1.4.3 the ability to respond positively to foreseeable changes in technology, working methods, markets and employment patterns and practices;

1.4.4 the underpinning skill, knowledge and understanding which is required for effective performance in employment.

1.5 Where areas of competence are common to a number of employment sectors, Lead Bodies will be expected to use **generic** units of competence whenever possible. These will often be produced by appropriate cross-sectoral Lead Bodies.

1.6 Lead Bodies should also consider making explicit their requirements for transferable **core skills** in areas such as communication, problem-solving and personal skills. The identification of such requirements in NVQs may become essential at a later date.

## 2 Format of NVQ statement of competence

The NVQ statement of competence, which is the authoritative statement of the national standard of performance, must have the following components:

2.1 **NVQ title**, agreed by NVQ, which denotes the area of competence encompassed by the qualification, and locates it in the NVQ framework;

2.2 **units of competence** are the main sub-divisions of an NVQ and consist of a coherent group of elements of competence which has meaning and independent value in the area of employment to which the NVQ statement of competence relates. An NVQ statement of competence will always have more than one unit.

    2.2.1 units must be designed so that they can be offered for separate assessment and certification, enabling them to be recorded as credits in the national credit accumulation and transfer system;

    2.2.2 units should have titles which indicate the sub-areas of competence they cover.

2.3 **Elements of competence** are the sub-divisions of units and reflect those things a person should be able to do at work. They should:

    2.3.1 relate to what actually happens in work and not, for example, activities or skills which are only demonstrated on training programmes;

    2.3.2 be capable of demonstration and assessment;

    2.3.3 describe the result of what is done, not the procedures which may be used;

    2.3.4 not contain evaluative statements – these belong in performance criteria (see below);

    2.3.5 be expressed in language which makes sense to the people who will use them and which is unambiguous;

2.3.6 be expressed in terms which permit application across different tasks, jobs, machines or organisational systems.

2.4 **Performance criteria** must accompany each element of competence and must contain evaluative statements which define the acceptable level of performance required in employment, normally in terms of its outcome, although some aspects of the way an activity is performed may also be critical. Performance criteria should:

2.4.1 identify only the essential aspects of performance necessary for competence;

2.4.2 be expressed so that assessments of candidates' peformance can be made against them;

2.4.3 form an unambiguous basis for the design of assessment systems and materials;

2.5 A **range statement** must also accompany each element. This should express the range of circumstances in which the competence must be applied, and may detail, for example, differences in physical location, employment contexts or machinery used.

2.6 **Assessment guidance**, although not part of the statement of competence, should also be provided by Lead Bodies for each element. In particular:

2.6.1 where candidates may not be able to present sufficient evidence of competence through performance alone, it will often be necessary to collect evidence of their possession of the essential underpinning knowledge and understanding. Lead Bodies should help awarding bodies and providers to interpret their requirements by indicating what knowledge and understanding is considered essential;

2.6.2 where it may be impossible or uneconomic to assess

performance across the whole of the range specified, the Lead Body should indicate the minimum requirements for performance evidence.

# 3 The NVQ framework

3.1 The NVQ framework is the national system for ordering NVQs according to progressive levels of attainment and areas of competence. It provides a structure for accredited qualifications which indicates the relationship between them and helps identify progression routes.

3.2 The NVQ framework currently has five levels – the following definitions are intended to be indicative rather than prescriptive:

**Level I:** competence in the performance of a range of varied work activities, most of which are routine and predictable *or* which provide a broad foundation as a basis for progression.

**Level II:** competence in a significant range of varied work activities, performed in a variety of contexts. Some of the activities are complex or non-routine, and there is some individual responsibility or autonomy. Collaboration with others, perhaps through membership of a work group or team, may often be a requirement.

**Level III:** competence in a broad range of varied work activities performed in a wide variety of contexts and most of which are complex and non-routine. There is considerable responsibility and autonomy, and control or guidance of others is often required.

**Level IV:** competence in a broad range of complex, technical or professional work activities performed in a wide variety of contexts and with a substantial degree of personal responsibility and autonomy. Responsibility for the work of others and the allocation of resources is often present.

**Level V:** competence which involves the application of a

significant range of fundamental principles and complex techniques across a wide and often unpredictable variety of contexts. Personal accountabilities for analysis and diagnosis, design, planning, execution and evaluation feature strongly, as do very substantial personal autonomy and often significant responsibility for the work of others and for the allocation of substantial resources.

3.3 The design of qualifications should take account of the following criteria:

3.3.1 direct comparability of standards and levels will be required between similar or adjacent occupational areas. Comparison across a wider range of occupations will be less exact, but the titles and levels of awards should express general levels of attainment which are universally understood;

3.3.2 not all occupational areas will require all five levels – the NCVQ will decide the level of an award based on the advice of lead and awarding bodies, the above definitions and the position of awards in similar areas of competence;

3.3.3 NVQs should be constructed so that candidates can progress from one level to the next and to related or adjacent areas of competence. It is not a requirement that all candidates progress through all levels – many will acquire the competences needed for NVQs at higher levels through learning programmes which lead directly to them;

3.3.4 NVQs may be made up of core units, which are common to a number of NVQs, and units which are specific to a single NVQ.

3.4 The NVQ framework provides a basis for making comparisons with qualifications from other European member states. This will enable NVQs to feature in future EEC comparability information and provide the basis for future dialogue on converging European standards.

3.5 The NVQ has developed a classification of areas of competence which will form the horizontal axis of the national framework; qualification titles and structures will increasingly be required to conform to this.

# 4 Assessment

4.1 Assessment for NVQs must be based on the statement of competence and the related assessment guidance. It is the process of collecting evidence and making judgements on whether or not performance criteria have been met. Before an NVQ can be awarded, candidates must have provided evidence that they have met the performance criteria for each element of competence specified.

4.2 Access to assessment for an NVQ should be available to all who have the potential to reach the standard required and be free from any barriers which restrict access. For example, assessment must be independent of:
- the mode or location of learning;
- upper and lower age limit, except where legal restraints make this necessary;
- a specified period of time to be spent in education, training or work.

4.3 The NCVQ requires that:

4.3.1 the method of assessment used in any circumstances is valid and reliable;

4.3.2 alternative forms of assessment are provided where this will help to increase access to the qualification;

4.3.3 performance evidence should feature in the assessments for all elements of an NVQ;

4.3.4 performance must be demonstrated and assessed

under conditions as close as possible to those under which it would normally be practised – preferably in the workplace;

4.3.5 if assessment in the workplace is not practicable, simulations, tests, projects or assignments may provide suitable evidence – but care must be taken to ensure that all elements and performance criteria have been covered, and that it is possible to predict that the competence assessed can be sustained in employment;

4.3.6 where performance evidence alone is limited and does not permit reliable inference of the possession of necessary knowledge and understanding, this must be separately assessed;

4.3.7 the method of assessment should always enable eligible candidates to demonstrate competence, and place no unnecessary additional demands on them;

4.3.8 some of the assessment for an NVQ may be conducted in a language other than English, provided that clear evidence is available that the candidate is competent in English to the standard required for competent performance throughout the UK;

4.3.9 provision should be made for the assessment of candidates with special needs, such as physical or sensory disabilities, who may need special help to undertake assessment. Where disabilities prevent candidates acquiring all the competences needed for the full NVQ, provision should be made for unit certification as appropriate;

4.3.10 a reliable system should be in place for recording evidence across the full range of circumstances in which the competence must be applied, as specified in the range statement.

## 5 Awarding bodies

5.1 The NCVQ approves bodies to award specific NVQs – it does not award them itself.

5.2 The NCVQ has the following general policies towards awarding bodies, in pursuit of its aims of rationalising and simplifying the system of vocational qualifications:

5.2.1 all NVQs in a given area of competence and at the same level must consist of a single national employment-led statement of competence provided by the appropriate Lead Body;

5.2.2 The NCVQ will encourage awarding bodies to develop their provision so that unnecessary duplication and overlap is avoided;

5.2.3 all bodies approved to award NVQs must particpate in the NCVQ's system of credit accumulation and transfer.

5.3 An NVQ may be awarded by a single body, or a consortium of relevant bodies acting together: where a consortium is involved, the NCVQ will require a clear statement of the contributions to be made to the process of awarding the NVQ by each of the bodies concerned prior to accreditation. Single bodies or consortia must:

5.3.1 have recognised standing with appropriate employers and representatives of employees (including trades unions) in respect of the awards proposed for accreditation as shown by their acceptability within the relevant occupational group, sector of industry, commerce of public service, or profession;

5.3.2 provide assessment throughout England and Wales. Separate arrangements may be made for Northern Ireland;

5.3.3 undertake to contribute to the maintenance of the

quality and relevance of the statements of competence which form part of the qualifications for which they seek accreditation;

5.3.4 agree to work with NCVQ and the Lead Bodies responsible for setting employment-led standards in the development and implementation of the NVQ framework;

5.3.5 be responsible for, and demonstrate capability in, the range of assessment required;

5.3.6 be responsible for the certification and administration of NVQs, including arrangements for credit accumulation and transfer;

5.3.7 have an equal opportunities policy and a means of monitoring its implementation; the policy and arrangements must be clearly communicated to candidates and to organisations involved in the delivery of training and education leading to the awards;

5.3.8 apply appropriate quality-assurance mechanisms;

5.3.9 agree to meet the conditions, regulations and guidelines specified or issued by the NCVQ from time to time for accredited qualifications and awarding bodies, and pay the appropriate fees promptly to the NCVQ.

## 6 Quality assurance

The NCVQ has an overriding responsibility for ensuring that awarding bodies have adequate arrangements and resources for quality assurance and that systems approved at the time of accreditation operate effectively and maintain the required performance throughout the period of accreditation. It will therefore require awarding bodies to have satisfactory arrangements for:

6.1 ensuring the competence of assessors;

6.2 monitoring or veryifying that assessment is operated in accordance with their requirements, and consistently maintained at all assessment locations;

6.3 selecting, training and reviewing the performance of moderators/verifiers;

6.4 instituting monitoring arrangements providing evidence of the effectiveness of their quality-assurance systems;

6.5 commissioning outside agencies to undertake evaluation where appropriate;

6.6 permitting NCVQ staff to attend meetings and/or training sessions for moderators/verifiers and assessors, and to see assessments taking place;

6.7 approving centres within which assessment will take place and ensuring they are capable of meeting all the requirements of the NVQ with regard to access, assessment and quality assurance;

6.8 administering, implementing, supporting and coordinating the above arrangements.

# 7 Accreditation

7.1 Accreditation is the procedure by which the NCVQ:

- approves an **NVQ statement of competence** agreed by an appropriate Lead Body in an area of competence and at a level in the NVQ framework;
- approves an **awarding body** to offer, administer and maintain the quality of NVQs;
- approves awarding arrangements for specific NVQs, which may involve consortia of awarding bodies.

7.2 Awarding bodies must demonstrate to the satisfaction of the NCVQ that the qualification they submit meet the criteria in parts 1–7 of this publication, and must accept contractually standard conditions which oblige them to:

7.2.1 include on each certificate awarded the designation 'National Vocational Qualification', the agreed title, the area of competence covered, the level in the NVQ framework, the names of all bodies associated with the award, the date of the award, and the NCVQ insignia;

7.2.2 ensure that each candidate completing the requirements for an NVQ is awarded a certificate in the agreed form. No other certificate should be issued in respect of the NVQ;

7.2.3 issue separate certificates (records of achievement) for units in the agreed form for the purpose of credit accumulation;

7.2.4 observe such regulations, guidelines and criteria as may be issued by the NCVQ in relation to the accredited award;

7.2.5 take all necessary steps to maintain the quality of the qualification by monitoring the assessment of candidates and other appropriate means;

7.2.6 maintain, in collaboration with other relevant bodies, the award's relevance to employment needs, and not make any material change in its specification without the NCVQ's approval;

7.2.7 pay such fee to the NCVQ per certificate awarded as may be agreed in respect of each NVQ.

7.3 In addition, the NCVQ may require awarding bodies to meet **specific conditions** by agreeing a plan to introduce changes in an NVQ over a defined period.

7.4 Accreditation may be given for a maximum period of five years; but where specific conditions are attached, the period may be shorter.

7.5 Awarding bodies may apply for **re-accreditation** shortly before the expiry of the period of accreditation; in addition to examining applications against all the criteria in parts 1–5, the NCVQ will also consider awarding bodies' general performance in quality assurance, contract compliance and fee payment.

# Details of Industry Lead Bodies

| Sector | Lead body | Coverage |
| --- | --- | --- |
| **Accountancy** | Mr P T Robinson<br>Chairman<br>Accountancy Working Party<br>Personnel Operations Manager<br>British Gas Plc<br>59 Bryanstone Street<br>London<br>W1A 2AZ<br>(Tel: 071 723 7030) | Accounting<br>Technicians<br>levels 2–4 |
| **Agriculture** | Mr J Sartain<br>Agricultural Training Board<br>Summit House<br>Glebe Way<br>West Wickham<br>Kent<br>BR4 0RF<br>(Tel: 081 777 9003) | Agricultural and<br>commercial<br>horticultural<br>services |
| **Air Transport** | Mr A J Hines<br>Aviation Training Association<br>125 London Road<br>High Wycombe<br>Bucks<br>HP11 1BT<br>(Tel: 0494 445262) | Air transport<br>services including<br>group support<br>staff |

| Sector | Lead body | Coverage |
|---|---|---|
| **Amenity Horticulture** | Richard Masters<br>LGTB<br>Arndale House<br>Arndale Centre<br>Luton<br>LU1 2TS<br>(Tel: 0582 451166) | All aspects of non-commercial horticulture |
| **Animal care** | Mr P Mann<br>Chairman Animal Care Lead<br>   Industry Body<br>White Chapel Way<br>Priorslee<br>Telford<br>Shropshire<br>TF2 0PQ<br>(Tel: 0952 290999) | Pet shops, catteries, kennels, groomers and zoos, veterinary practices |
| **Architecture and professional bodies in construction** | CISC<br>Mr A Osborne<br>The Building Centre<br>26 Store Street<br>London<br>WC1E 7BT<br>(Tel: 071 33 5270) | Architecture, building and quantity surveying building and civil engineering |
| **Armed forces** | to be established | |
| **Arts and performing arts** | Arts Council of Great Britain<br>14 Great Peter Street<br>London<br>SW1P 3NQ<br>(Tel: 071 973 6590) | |
| **Baking** | Mr S P Watson<br>Federation of Bakers<br>20 Bedford Square<br>London<br>WC1B 3HF<br>(Tel: 071 637 7575) | Large process baking bread/flour confectionery production and distribution |

| Sector | Lead body | Coverage |
| --- | --- | --- |
| | Mr D Harbourne<br>National Association of<br>   Master Bakers,<br>   Confectioners and Caterers<br>21 Baldock Street<br>Ware<br>Herts<br>SH12 9DH<br>(Tel: 0920 68061) | Small bakers |
| | Mr I Hay<br>Scottish Association of<br>   Master Bakers<br>Athol House<br>4 Tropichen Street<br>Edinburgh<br>EH3 8JQ<br>(Tel: 031 229 1401) | As above in<br>Scotland |
| **Banking** | Banking Lead Body<br>Nicholas Fox<br>Room E501<br>Training Agency<br>Moorfoot<br>Sheffield<br>S1 4PQ<br>(Tel: 0742 539470) | |
| **Basket making** | Mrs O Elton-Barratt<br>The Basket Makers Association<br>Millfield Cottage<br>Little Hadham<br>Ware<br>Herts<br>SG11 2ED<br>(Tel: 0279 51497) | Manufacture<br>Baskets and Allied<br>Products using<br>natural materials |

| Sector | Lead body | Coverage |
| --- | --- | --- |
| **Biscuit, cake, chocolate etc** | Mr M J Webber<br>Biscuit, Cake, Chocolate and<br>    Confectionary Alliance<br>11 Green Street<br>London<br>W1Y 3RF<br>(Tel: 071 629 8971) | Manufacture of<br>biscuits, cakes,<br>cocoa, chocolate<br>and sugar<br>confectionery |
| **Blacksmiths** | Ms S Jagger<br>Nations Association of Farriers,<br>    Blacksmiths and Agricultural<br>    Engineers<br>Avenue R 7th Street<br>NEC<br>Stoneleigh<br>Warwickshire<br>CV8 2LG<br>(Tel: 0203 696595) | Craftsmanship and<br>'artist'<br>craftsmanship;<br>small business<br>competences |
| **Boat building** | Mr P Wagstaff<br>British Marine Industries<br>    Federation<br>Boating Industry House<br>Vale Road<br>Oatlands Park<br>Weybridge<br>Surrey KT13 9NS<br>(Tel: 0932 854511) | Boat building |
| **Books** | Mr D Smith<br>Bookhouse Training Centre<br>45 East Hill<br>Wandsworth<br>London<br>SW18 2QZ<br>(Tel: 081 874 2718) | Book publishing |

| Sector | Lead body | Coverage |
|--------|-----------|----------|
| **Brushes** | Mr H Nisbett<br>British Brush Manufacturers<br>   Association<br>35 Billing Road<br>Northampton<br>NN1 5DD<br>(Tel: 0604 22023) | Brush manufacture |
| **Building maintenance and estate management** | Mr K Owen<br>Institute of Maintenance and<br>   Building Management<br>Keets House<br>30 East Street<br>Farnham<br>Surrey<br>GU9 7SW<br>(Tel: 0252 710994) | Maintenance and servicing of buildings, estates, industrial and commercial properties |
| **Building societies** | Mr G Yates<br>Chairman – Building Society<br>   Lead Body<br>Yorkshire Building Society<br>Yorkshire House<br>Westgate<br>Bradford<br>BD1 2AU<br>(Tel: 0274 734822) | All aspects of building societies |
| **Bus & coach** | M J Jones<br>Bus and Coach Training Limited<br>Gable House<br>40 High Street<br>Rickmansworth<br>WD3 1ER<br>(Tel: 0923 896607) | Bus & coach operations |

| Sector | Lead body | Coverage |
| --- | --- | --- |
| **Business Administration (secretarial)** | Mr F Fenton<br>Chairman<br>National Working Party for<br>    Secretarial Standards<br>The Electricity Council<br>Room 517<br>Industrial Relations Dept<br>30 Millbank<br>London<br>SW1P 4RD<br>(Tel: 071 834 2333) | Generic and specialist secretarial and administrative occupations (NCVQ levels 3 and 4) |
| **Care** | P Martin<br>The Secretariat<br>Care Sector Consortium<br>    (NHSTA)<br>St Bartholomews Court<br>18 Christmas Street<br>Bristol<br>BS1 5BT<br>(Tel: 0272 291029) | Public and private sectors of health and social services and voluntary sector |
| **Carpets** | Mr B Hull<br>Carpet Industry Training Council<br>39 Knox Chase<br>Harrogate<br>HG1 3HL<br>(Tel: Voicebank 042 698 9880)<br>(Part of National Textile Training Group) | Carpet manufacture |
| **Caravanning and leisure parks** | Caroline Cawley<br>Caravan Industry Training<br>    Organisation<br>88 Victoria Road<br>Aldershot<br>Hants<br>GU11 1SS<br>(Tel: 0252 344170) | Selling of caravans/operations of caravan parks |

| Sector | Lead body | Coverage |
| --- | --- | --- |
| **Cement** | Dr G C Bye<br>British Cement Association<br>Wexham Springs<br>Slough<br>SL3 6PL<br>(Tel: 0753 662727) | Cement manufacture and distribution |
| | R Barry<br>Fibre Cement Manufacturers<br>  Association<br>PO Box 92<br>Elmswell<br>Bury St Edmunds<br>Suffolk<br>IP30 9HS<br>(Tel: 0359 259379) | Manufacture of fibre cement and building materials made from asbestos and asbestos substitute |
| **Ceramics** | Mr B Leader<br>Ceramics Industry Training<br>  Organisation<br>Cornwall House<br>Sandy Lane<br>Newcastle Under Lyme<br>Staffs<br>ST5 0LZ<br>(Tel: 0782 638755) | Ceramic goods manufacture |
| **Chemicals** | Mr K G McNichol<br>Chemical Industry Association<br>Kings Building<br>Smith Square<br>London<br>SW1P 3JJ<br>(Tel: 071 834 3399) | Chemical manufacture |

| Sector | Lead body | Coverage |
| --- | --- | --- |
| **Chimney sweeps** | Mr D Malkin<br>National Association of Chimney<br>   Sweeps<br>PO Box 35<br>Stoke on Trent<br>Staffordshire<br>ST4 7NU<br>(Tel: 0782 744311) | Practitioners;<br>small business<br>competences |
| **Civil Service** | Mr D Wood<br>Cabinet Office (OMCS)<br>Deputy Head of Division<br>Training Development Division<br>11 Belgrave Road<br>London<br>SW1V 1RB | All aspects of Civil<br>Service |
| **Clay pipes and refractories** | Mr G Baker Director<br>Refractories, Clay Pipes and<br>   Allied Industries Training<br>   Council<br>c/o The University of Sheffield<br>School of Materials<br>Elmfield<br>Northumberland Road<br>Sheffield<br>S10 2TZ<br>(Tel: 0742 768555 Ext 6093) | Manufacture of<br>refractories, clay<br>pipes, abrasives<br>and carbon<br>electrodes |
| **Cleaning** | Mr M Bizley<br>ISS Servisystem Ltd<br>95 Albert Street<br>Birmingham<br>B5 5LN<br>(Tel: 021 643 8831) | |

| Sector | Lead body | Coverage |
|---|---|---|
| **Clothing** | Ms H France/Mr G Browning<br>Clothing and Allied Products<br>   Industry Training Board<br>80 Richardshaw Lane<br>Pudsey<br>Leeds<br>LS28 6BN<br>(Tel: 0532 393355) | Manufacture of<br>clothing and allied<br>products from<br>materials |
| **Concrete** | Mr M King<br>Autoclaved Aerated Concrete<br>   Products Association<br>Tarmac Toplock Ltd<br>Roadstone House<br>PO Box 44<br>50 Waterloo Road<br>Wolverhampton<br>WV1 4RU<br>(Tel: 0902 754131) | Manufacture of<br>aerated concrete<br>products |
| | A R Wilson<br>Pre-Cast Concrete Industry<br>   Training Association<br>60 Charles Street<br>Leicester<br>LE1 1FB<br>(Tel: 0533 20607) | Manufacture of<br>pre-cast concrete<br>products |
| **Conservation of Environment** | Mr Keith Turner<br>COSQUEC<br>The Red House<br>Pillows Green<br>Staunton<br>Gloucs<br>GL19 3NU<br>(Tel: 045 284505) | Land-based<br>industries and<br>urban conservation |

| Sector | Lead body | Coverage |
|---|---|---|
| **Construction** | Construction Industry Training Board<br>24–30 West Smithfield<br>London<br>EC1A 9JA<br>(Tel: 071 489 1662) | All aspects of construction |
| **Cosmetics** | To be established | |
| **Cotton and allied products** | Mr B Bruce<br>CATITO<br>Reedham House<br>31 King Street West<br>Manchester<br>M3 2PF<br>(Tel: 061 832 9291) | Manufacture of cotton and allied products |
| **Crafts and enterprise** | To be established | Crafts, design for crafts; small business competences |
| **Dairy** | Mr N Spencer<br>Dairy Trade Federation<br>19 Cornwall Terrace<br>London<br>NW1 4QP<br>(Tel: 071 486 7244) | Production, distribution and retailing of dairy products |
| **Design** | To be established | |
| **Drinks** | Mr J Edgar<br>Drinks Industries Training Association<br>42 Portman Square<br>London<br>W1H 0BB<br>(Tel: 071 352 1326) | Manufacture and distribution of alcoholic drinks other than whisky |

| Sector | Lead body | Coverage |
| --- | --- | --- |
| | Mr H Houghton<br>British Soft Drinks Association<br>6 Catherine Street<br>London<br>WC2B 5UA<br>(Tel: 071 379 5737) | Manufacture of<br>soft drinks and<br>mineral water |
| **Dry cleaners** | Noel Goldthorp<br>The Textile, Retail, Dry<br>   Cleaning, Laundering & Allied<br>   Services Industry Lead Body<br>c/o Fabric Care Research<br>   Association Ltd<br>Forest House Laboratories<br>Knaresborough Road<br>Harrogate<br>North Yorkshire<br>NG2 7LZ<br>(Tel: 0423 885977) | Dry clearners<br>launderers and<br>pressers |
| **Education** | To be established | |
| **Electrical contracting** | Mr John Walker<br>Director<br>Joint Industry Board for the<br>   Electrical Contracting<br>   Industry<br>Kingswood House<br>47/51 Sidcup Hill<br>Sidcup<br>Kent<br>DA14 6NP<br>(Tel: 081 302 0031) | Electrical<br>contracting in the<br>construction<br>industry |
| | Mr E Kendrick<br>Training Education Manager<br>Electricity Training Association<br>30 Millbank<br>London<br>SW1P 4RD<br>(Tel: 071 384 2333) | |

| Sector | Lead body | Coverage |
|---|---|---|
| **Electrical Services** | To be established | |
| **Electricity** | Mr E Kendrick<br>Electricity Council Industrial<br>   Relations Dept<br>30 Millbank<br>London<br>SW1 4RD<br>(Tel: 071 834 2333) | Public electricity<br>supply |
| **Electronic office (Maintenance and Systems)** | Mr J Bache<br>Electronic Office Equipment<br>   Servicing ILB<br>37 Moor Park Road<br>Northwood<br>Middlesex<br>HA6 2DH | Servicing office<br>equipment |
| **Energy Management** | To be established | |
| **Engineering** | Mr E Pennant Jones<br>Engineering Industry Training<br>   Board<br>PO Box 176<br>54 Clarendon Road<br>Watford<br>Herts<br>WD1 1LB<br>(Tel: 0923 38441) | Engineering<br>industry and<br>related trades |
| **Engineering construction** | Mr D Roy<br>ECI Sector<br>PO Box 148<br>41 Clarendon Road<br>Watford<br>Herts<br>WD1 1HS<br>(Tel: 0923 38441) | Engineering<br>construction |

| Sector | Lead body | Coverage |
| --- | --- | --- |
| **Engineering Professional bodies** | To be established | |
| **Envelope makers** | M L Pagliero OBE RCIS<br>Envelope Makers and<br>    Manufacturing Stationers<br>    Association<br>44 St Martin's Approach<br>Ruislip<br>Middlesex<br>HA7 7OQ<br>(Tel: 0895 632867) | Manufacturing of envelopes and paper stationery |
| **Estate agents** | Colin Charlesworth<br>Estate Agency Training Group<br>E501<br>Training Agency<br>Moorfoot<br>Sheffield<br>S1 4PQ<br>(Tel: 0742 593672) | |
| **Extractive industries** | Dr G G Wilkinson<br>Quarry Products Training<br>    Council<br>27 Crendon Street<br>High Wycombe<br>Bucks<br>HP13 6LJ<br>(Tel: 0494 34124) | Quarry products |
| | M Gowan<br>China and Ball Clay Industry<br>    Training Board<br>John Keay House<br>St Austell<br>Cornwall<br>PL25 4DJ<br>(Tel: 0726 74482) | China and ball clay extraction |

| Sector | Lead body | Coverage |
| --- | --- | --- |
| | M Adcock<br>Silica and Moulding Sands<br>    Association<br>19 Warwick Street<br>Rugby<br>Warwickshire<br>CV21 3DH<br>(Tel: 078 73041) | Excavation and<br>processing of<br>sands required for<br>glass production<br>and machining in<br>steel works |
| **Fibre board<br>and packing** | Mrs Glynis Richards<br>British Fibreboards and<br>    Packing Assoc<br>2 Saxon Court<br>Freeschool Street<br>Northampton<br>NN1 1ST | Production of fibre<br>board and<br>packaging<br>materials |
| **Film making** | Ms H Coote<br>The Independent Media Training<br>    Federation<br>The National Film and Television<br>    School<br>Beaconsfield Studios<br>Station Road<br>Beaconsfield<br>Bucks<br>HP9 1LG | |
| **Fire service** | Mr B Hogg<br>Chairman – Fire Lead Body<br>Nuclear Electric<br>Sudbury House<br>Courtney House<br>Room 921<br>15 Newgate Street<br>London<br>E1A 7AU | |

| Sector | Lead body | Coverage |
| --- | --- | --- |
| **Flexible packaging** | Flexible Packaging Association<br>4 The Street<br>Shipton Moyne<br>Tetbury<br>Gloucestershire<br>GL8 8PN | Production of flexible packaging |
| **Floristry** | Mrs E Hart<br>Floristry Industry Vocational<br>    Qualifications Group<br>Tottenham College of Technology<br>High Road<br>Tottenham<br>London<br>N15 4RU<br>(Tel: 081 802 3111) | Preparation and sale of flowers and shubbery for display and decoration |
| **Food manufacture** | Mrs M Hiley<br>Food Manufacturers Council<br>    for Industrial Training<br>6 Catherine Street<br>London<br>WC2B 5JJ<br>(Tel: 071 836 2460) | Food manufacture |
| | Mr M D Defrates<br>UK Association of Frozen<br>    Food Products<br>1 Green Street<br>London<br>W1Y 3RG<br>(Tel: 071 629 0655) | Production of frozen foods and ice-cream |
| **Footwear manufacture** | Mr M J R Heron<br>British Footwear<br>    Manufacturers Federation<br>Royalty House<br>72 Dean Street<br>London<br>W1V 5HB<br>(Tel: 071 734 0951) | Footwear manufacture |

| Sector | Lead body | Coverage |
| --- | --- | --- |
| **Footware repair** | Mr A R Hudson c/o Freeman, Hardy & Willis 45 Briggate Leeds LS1 5HD (Tel: 0532 452266) | Shoe repairs by multiple operators |
| **Forensic science** | To be established | |
| **Forestry** | Mr Robertson Forestry Training Council Room 413 231 Corstorphine Road Edinburgh EH12 7AT (Tel: 031 334 0303) | Forestry work, harvesting, arboriculture, silviculture |
| **Fresh produce** | Mr G Eugster National Institute of Fresh Produce 111 Market Towers 1 Nine Elms Lane London SW8 5NQ (Tel: 071 720 4465) | Distribution and retailing of fruit vegetables and flowers |
| **Furniture** | Mr D Freeland Secretary British Furniture Manufacturing Federation 30 Harcourt Street London W1H 2AA (Tel: 071 724 0854) (Part of Furniture and Timber Sector Consultative Group) | Furniture manufacture |

| Sector | Lead body | Coverage |
|---|---|---|
| **Gamekeeping and fish husbandry** | Mr J Shaw<br>Joint Council for Gamekeeping and Fish Husbandry<br>Hampshire College of Agriculture<br>Sparsholt<br>Nr Winchester<br>Hampshire | All aspects of fish husbandry and gamekeeping |
| **Garden and Agricultural Machinery** | Ms W Bridgeman<br>British Agricultural and Garden Machinery Association<br>Church Street<br>Rickmansworth<br>Herts<br>WD3 1 RQ<br>(Tel: 0923 720241) | Agricultural and garden machinery |
| **Gas** | Mr J C Bailey<br>British Gas<br>326 High Holborn<br>London<br>WC1<br>(Tel: 071 723 7030) | Public gas supply and extraction |
| **Glass** | Mr H Hearsum<br>Glass Training Ltd<br>BGMC Building<br>Northumberland Road<br>Sheffield<br>S10 2UA<br>(Tel: 0742 661494/669263) | Glass and glass products manufacture, glass processing and installation |
| **Guidance and counselling** | To be established | Guidance outside education sector |

| Sector | Lead body | Coverage |
|---|---|---|
| **Hairdressing** | A Goldsbro<br>Hairdressing Training Board<br>Silver House<br>Silver Street<br>Doncaster<br>DN1 1HL<br>(Tel: 0302 342837) | All aspects of hairdressing and hair care |
| **Hand and machine knitting** | Mrs D Davies<br>British School of Knitting<br>6–16, 18–20 Laugston Studios<br>Kingham<br>Oxon<br>OX7 6UP<br>(Tel: 0608 643894) | Pattern leaflet production manufacture by:<br>a) Hand Knitting;<br>b) semi-industrial machines;<br>c) domestic knitting machines;<br>d) crochet work, spinning, dyeing |
| **Health & beauty** | Mr W Sharps<br>HBTTB<br>PO Box 21<br>Bognor Regis<br>West Sussex<br>PO22 7PS<br>(Tel: 0243 860339) | Suntanning operators, electrolysists, trichologists, alstricticians, aestheticians, cosmetology |
| **Health & safety** | To be established | Health and safety practitioners |
| **Horses** | Col John Goldsmith<br>Joint National Horse Education<br>    and Training Council<br>British Horse Society<br>Stoneleigh<br>Warwickshire<br>(Tel: 0203 696697) | All aspects of horse world |

DETAILS OF INDUSTRY LEAD BODIES

| Sector | Lead body | Coverage |
|---|---|---|
| **Hotel & catering** | Dr Anne Walker<br>Hotel and Catering Training Board<br>International House<br>High Street<br>Ealing<br>London<br>W5 5DB<br>(Tel: 081 579 2400) | All aspects of hotel and catering work |
| **Housing** | Mr Tony Smith<br>LGTB (for Housing Sector Consortium)<br>Arndale House<br>The Arndale Centre<br>Luton<br>LU1 2TS<br>(Tel: 0582 451166) | All aspects of housing, (except building) rental, allocation, finance |
| **Information technology** | Mr B J Gibbens<br>Chairman<br>Information Technology industry Lead Body<br>SEMA Group Plc<br>22 Long Acre<br>London<br>WC2E 9LY | Practitioners, constructive users, and office and IT equipment maintenance |
| **Information Technology constructive users** | Mr J S Fisher<br>ITILB Constructive User Group<br>IT Centre<br>Vickers Shipbuilding & Engineering Ltd<br>Training Division<br>Engineering Works<br>Barrow-in-Furness<br>Cumbria | |

| Sector | Lead body | Coverage |
| --- | --- | --- |
| **Information technology practitioners** | Mr M Ould<br>ITILB Practitioner Sub-group<br>Praxis Systems<br>20 Manvers Street<br>Bath<br>BA1 1PX | |
| **Information technology qualifications** | Mr A Allen<br>ITILB Qualifications Sub-group<br>Director of Information<br>   Processing Services<br>Tayside Regional Council<br>Tayside House<br>Crighton Street<br>Dundee | |
| **Inland waterways** | Mr C Webb<br>British Waterways Board<br>Willow Grange<br>Church Road<br>Watford<br>WD1 3QA<br>(Tel: 0923 226422) | Inland water transport, working waterways, leisure |
| **Insurance** | Mr H Parry<br>Insurance Industry Training<br>   Council<br>Churchill Court<br>90 Kippington Road<br>Sevenoaks<br>Kent<br>TN13 2LL<br>(Tel: 0732 450801) | Insurance services |

| Sector | Lead body | Coverage |
|---|---|---|
| **International trade** | Mrs B Fletcher<br>International Trade and<br>   Services Industry Lead Body<br>Institute of Chartered<br>   Shipbrokers<br>24 St Mary Axe<br>London<br>EC3A 8DE | |
| **Jewellery** | Ms G Packard<br>National Joint Working Group<br>   for the Jewellery & Allied<br>   Industries<br>British Jewellers Association<br>St Dunstan's House<br>Cavey Lane<br>London<br>EC2V 8AA<br>(Tel: 071 437 5902) | Stone set jewellery; precious metal jewellery, metal fashion jewellery, silverware, pewter, medals, cutlery |
| **Knitting and lace** | Ms J Long<br>Knitting and Lace Industries<br>   Training Resource Agency<br>Gregory Boulevard<br>Nottingham<br>NH 6NB<br>(Tel: 0602 623311)<br>(Now part of National Textile<br>Training Group) | All aspects of knitting and lace manufacture |
| **Languages** | Language Lead Body<br>c/o CILT (Centre for<br>   Information on Language<br>   Teaching and Research<br>Regent's College<br>Regent's Park<br>London<br>NW1 4NS | |

| Sector | Lead body | Coverage |
| --- | --- | --- |
| Law | To be established | |
| Leather processing | Mr J Purvis<br>British Leather Confederation<br>Leather Trade House<br>Kings Park Road<br>Moulton Park<br>Northampton<br>NN3 1JD<br>(Tel: 0604 494131) | Leather processing (preparation of hides and skins) |
| Light leather goods manufacture and factory production of saddles and bridles | Mr D Howard<br>Walsall Chamber of Commerce<br>    and Industry Training Division<br>St Paul's Road<br>Wood Green<br>Wednesbury<br>West Midlands<br>WS10 9QX<br>(Tel: 021 526 2071) | Manufacture of leather goods (except footwear) including factory production of saddles and bridles |
| Leather – saddle and bridle manufacture; leather crafts | Society of Master Saddlers<br>The Saddlers Company<br>40 Gutter Lane<br>London<br>EC2V 6BR<br><br>Mr Kingsley M Oliver<br>Clerk to the Company<br>Saddler's Company<br>Saddler's Hall<br>40 Gutter Lane<br>London<br>EC2V 6BR<br>(Tel: 071 726 8661/6) | Craft production of saddles and bridles |

| Sector | Lead body | Coverage |
|---|---|---|
| **Local government** | Mr R Taylor<br>Local Government Training Board<br>4th Floor<br>Arndale House<br>The Arndale Centre<br>Luton<br>LU1 2TS<br>(Tel: 0582 451166) | Local government services<br>(excluding police and fire services) |
| **Locksmiths** | Master Locksmiths Association<br>13 Parkfield Road<br>Northolt<br>Middlesex<br>UB5 5NN<br>(Tel: 071 242 8045) | Lock making and repair: small business competences |
| **Management and supervisory occupations** | Sir R Reid<br>Chairman<br>National Forum for Management<br>　Education Development<br>Shell Mex House<br>The Strand<br>London WC2<br>(Contacts: Mike Day/<br>　Pauline Watts<br>　071 257 3761/5952) | Management and supervisory occupations |
| **Management services** | Mr G Owen<br>Institute of Management<br>　Services<br>1 Cecil Court<br>London Road<br>Enfield<br>Middlesex<br>EN2 6DD | |

| Sector | Lead body | Coverage |
|---|---|---|
| **Man made fibres** | Mr P Grice<br>Man Made Fibres<br>Industry Training Advisory<br>  Board<br>Central House<br>Gate Lane<br>Sutton Coldfield<br>West Midlands<br>B73 5TS<br>(Tel: 021 355 7022) | Production of man made fibres |
| **Merchant navy** | Mr R C Matthew<br>Merchant Navy Training Board<br>30/32 St Mary Axe<br>London<br>EC3A 8ET<br>(Tel: 071 283 2922) | Merchant navy |
| **Meat** | Mr R Hotchkiss<br>Meat Industry Training<br>  Organisation<br>PO Box 661<br>Winterhill House<br>Snowdon Drive<br>Milton Keynes<br>MK6 1BB<br>(Tel: 0908 609829) | Meat & poultry products |
| **Millers** | Mr N Bennett<br>Incorporated National<br>  Association of British and<br>  Irish Millers<br>21 Arlington Street<br>London<br>SW1A 1RN<br>(Tel: 071 493 2521) | Grain milling production and distribution |
| **Mining (including coke)** | To be established | Coal mining |

| Sector | Lead body | Coverage |
|---|---|---|
| **Museums, Galleries and Heritage** | Simon Roodhouse<br>Museum Training Institute<br>Ground Floor<br>Kershaw House<br>55 Well Street<br>Bradford<br>BD1 5PS<br>(Tel: 0274 391092) | Museums, galleries and heritage work |
| **Narrow fabrics** | British Narrow Fabrics<br>  Association<br>4th Floor<br>York House<br>91 Granby Street<br>Leicester<br>LE1 6EA<br>(Tel: 0533 545490)<br>(Part of National Textile<br>Training Group) | Manufacture of ribbon, fabric tapes etc |
| **Newspapers** | Mr W Hird<br>Newspaper Publishers<br>  Association<br>84 Southwark Bridge Road<br>London<br>SE1 GEU<br>(Tel: 071 928 6928) | Fleet Street newspapers publishing and printing |
| | Mr G J Hartridge<br>Newspaper Society<br>Bloomsbury House<br>Bloomsbury Square<br>74–77 Great Russell Street<br>London<br>WC1B 30A<br>(Tel: 071 636 7014) | Regional newspapers, printing and publishing (England and Wales) |

| Sector | Lead body | Coverage |
|--------|-----------|----------|
| | Mr W Kidd<br>Society of Master Printers<br>of Scotland<br>48 Palmerston Place<br>Edinburgh<br>EH12 5DE<br>(Tel: 031 220 4353) | |
| **Nuclear** | Mr R Baines<br>British Nuclear Fuels<br>Risley<br>Warrington<br>WA3 6AS<br>(Tel: 0925 83200) | Nuclear fuel<br>production;<br>enrichment<br>processing and<br>waste management |
| | A P Springett<br>UK Atomic Energy Authority<br>11 Charles II Street<br>London<br>SW1Y 4QP<br>(Tel: 071 930 5454) | Research and<br>development for UK<br>nuclear programme |
| **Office skills** | Mr C Charlesworth<br>Administrative Business and<br>Commercial Training Group<br>E501<br>Training Agency<br>Moorfoot<br>Sheffield<br>S1 4PQ | All aspects of<br>office work (NCVQ<br>levels 1 and 2) |
| **Off shore oil** | Mr F Jenkins<br>Off Shore Petroleum Industry<br>Training Board<br>SCOTA Building<br>Blackness Avenue<br>Altens<br>Aberdeen<br>Scotland<br>AB1 4PG<br>(Tel: 0674 72230) | Exploration and<br>drilling for<br>production of<br>petroleum |

| Sector | Lead body | Coverage |
| --- | --- | --- |
| **Packaging** | Mr J M W Williams<br>National Packaging<br>　　Confederation<br>Woodhill Road<br>Danbury<br>Essex<br>CM3 4AL<br>(Tel: 024 561 4313) | Production of<br>packaging products |
| **Paint** | Mr D Clement<br>Paintmakers Association of<br>　　of Great Britain<br>6th Floor<br>Alembic House<br>93 Albert Embankment<br>London<br>SE1 7TY<br>(Tel: 071 582 1185) | Manufacture of<br>paints and<br>varnishes |
| **Paper and board** | Mr T Linley<br>British Paper and Board<br>　　Industry Federation<br>Papermakers House<br>Rivenhall Road<br>Westlea<br>Swindon<br>SN5 7BE<br>(Tel: 0793 886086) | Paper and board<br>manufacture |
| **Pensions management** | Mrs S M Howlett<br>The Pensions Management<br>　　Institute<br>PMI House<br>124 Middlesex Street<br>London<br>E1 7HY<br>(Tel: 071 247 1452<br>　Fax: 071 375 0603) | |

| Sector | Lead body | Coverage |
| --- | --- | --- |
| **Periodicals** | Mr A R Sumption<br>Periodicals Training Council<br>Imperial House<br>15–19 Kingsway<br>London<br>WC2 6UN<br>(Tel: 071 836 8798) | Publishing of<br>magazines and<br>journals |
| **Personnel management** | Mr A Durrant<br>Rm E501 Section QS7<br>Training Agency<br>Moorfoot<br>Sheffield<br>S1 4PQ | All aspects of<br>personnel<br>management except<br>training and<br>development |
| **Petrol refining** | Mr R J Barnard<br>Petroleum Training Federation<br>Room 326<br>162–168 Regent Street<br>London<br>W1R 5TL<br>(Tel: 071 439 2632) | Refining and<br>distribution of<br>petroleum products |
| **Pharma-ceuticals** | Mr P Smith<br>Association of the British<br>    Pharmaceutical Industry<br>12 Whitehall<br>London<br>SW1A 2HY<br>(Tel: 071 930 3477) | Manufacture of<br>prescription<br>medicines |
| **Photography** | Mr M Berry<br>Vocational Standards Council<br>    for the Photographic and<br>    Photographic Processing<br>    Industries<br>British Institute of Professional<br>    Photography<br>Amwell End | Skills photography<br>and associated<br>processing |

| Sector | Lead body | Coverage |
|--------|-----------|----------|
| | Ware<br>Herts<br>SG12 9HN<br>(Tel: 0920 464011) | |
| Police | Mr M Igoe<br>Training Agency<br>Rm E704A Section QS7<br>Moorfoot<br>Sheffield<br>S1 4PQ | All police<br>occupations |
| Ports and harbours | J Weekes<br>British Ports Federation<br>Victoria House<br>Vernon Place<br>London<br>WC1B 4LL<br>(Tel: 071 242 1200<br> Fax: 071 405 1069) | Support services<br>to sea transport |
| Post Office | Mr M McGinley<br>Post Office Management<br>  College<br>Coton House<br>Rugby<br>CV23 0AA | All Post Office<br>occupations |
| Plastics | Mr J Shearman<br>Plastics Processing Industry<br>  Training Board<br>Coppice House<br>Halesfield<br>Telford<br>Shropshire<br>TF7 4NA<br>(Tel: 0952 587020) | Processing of<br>plastics products<br>and materials |

| Sector | Lead body | Coverage |
|---|---|---|
| **Printing** | Mr A Keeble<br>British Printing Industries<br>　Federation<br>11 Bedford Row<br>London<br>WC1R 4DX<br>(Tel: 071 242 6904) | General printing |
| | Mr W Kidd<br>Society of Master Printers of<br>　Scotland<br>48 Palmerston Place<br>Edinburgh<br>EH12 5DE<br>(Tel: 031 220 4353) | General printing<br>and non-daily<br>newspapers in<br>Scotland |
| **Printing ink** | Mr P W G Seabrook<br>The Society of British Printing<br>　Ink Manufacturers Ltd<br>PIRA House<br>Randall's Road<br>Leatherhead<br>Surrey KT22 7RU<br>(Tel: 0372 378628) | Manufacture of<br>printing ink |
| **Prisons** | To be established | |
| **Purchasing and supply** | Mr C M G Allen CBE FInst PS<br>Chairman<br>Purchasing & Supply Lead Body<br>Institute of Purchasing &<br>　Supply<br>Easton House<br>Easton on the Hill<br>Stamford<br>Lincolnshire<br>PE9 3NZ<br>(Tel: 0780 56777) | |

| Sector | Lead body | Coverage |
| --- | --- | --- |
| **Railways** | Mr R M Evans<br>Railway Industry Lead Body<br>Training & Development Manager<br>　(Operations)<br>British Railways Board<br>Tournament House<br>Paddington Station<br>London W2 1HQ | Rail operations |
| **Retail** | Mr P Morley<br>Chairman<br>National Retail Training Council<br>3rd Floor<br>Trent House<br>69–79 Fulham High Street<br>London SW6<br>(Tel: 071 371 5021) | All aspects of retail trade & sub-sectors in drapery and fashion; DIY; food; wines and spirits; chemists and pharmacy; book sellers; radio and electrical, hardware jewellery; stationery, furniture and furnishings |
| **Retail travel** | Mr K Atkinson<br>Association of British Travel<br>　Agents National Training<br>　Board<br>Waterloo House<br>11–17 Chertsey Road<br>Woking<br>Surrey<br>GU21 5AJ<br>(Tel: 04862 27321) | Tour operation and travel agents |

| Sector | Lead body | Coverage |
|--------|-----------|----------|
| **Road transport** | Mr D Webber<br>Road Transport Industry<br>   Training Board<br>Capitol House<br>Empire Way<br>Wembley<br>Middlesex<br>HA9 0NG<br>(Tel: 081 902 8880) | Road haulage; vehicle hire; motor vehicle sales, service and repair; vehicle body building and repair; furniture removals; forecourt operations and motor factoring |
| **Rubber** | Mr J T Downing<br>British Rubber Industry Training<br>   Board<br>Scala House<br>Holloway Circus<br>Birmingham<br>B1 1EG<br>(Tel: 021 643 9599) | Processing, distribution, retailing of rubber material and manufacture of rubber products including reclaimed rubber |
| **Sales** | Mr Richard Berry<br>Direct Selling Assocaition<br>44 Russell Square<br>London<br>WC1B 4JP<br>(Tel: 071 580 8433) | |
| **Sea fishing** | Mr K D Waind<br>Sea Fish Authority Industrial<br>   Development Unit<br>St Andrew's Dock<br>Hull<br>HU3 4QE<br>(Tel: 0482 27837) | Commercial sea fishing, processing, wholesaling, retailing |
| **Security** | Mr E Parkinson MBE<br>Chairman<br>Security (Manned Services) ILB<br>9 Loukias Papageorgiou Street<br>Limasol<br>TT249<br>Cyprus | Manned services |

| Sector | Lead body | Coverage |
| --- | --- | --- |
| | Mr A Young QPM LLB<br>Company Security Adviser<br>Chairman<br>Security (Emergency Systems)<br>  ILB<br>J Sainsbury Plc<br>Stamford House<br>Stamford Street<br>London<br>SE1 9LL | Alarms |
| **Screen printers** | Mr M Turner<br>Display Producers & Screen<br>   Printers Association Limited<br>7a West Street<br>Reigate<br>Surrey<br>RH2 9BL<br>(Tel: 0737 240792) | All printing done by<br>screen technology<br>within three areas:<br>— general printing<br>— industrial and<br>  commercial<br>  printing<br>— textile printing |
| **Shipbuilding** | Mr L D Lubman<br>Marine Training Association<br>Rycote Place<br>30–38 Cambridge Street<br>Aylesbury<br>Bucks<br>HP20 1RS<br>(Tel: 0296 434943) | Shipbuilding and<br>repair |
| **Signmaking** | Mr P Tipton<br>British Sign Association<br>Swan House<br>207 Balham High Road<br>London<br>SW17 7BQ<br>(Tel: 081 675 7241) | Making signs |

| Sector | Lead body | Coverage |
| --- | --- | --- |
| **Soap & detergent** | Mr B K Chesterton<br>Soap and Detergent Association<br>PO Box 9<br>Hayes Gate House<br>Hayes<br>Middlesex<br>UB4 0JD<br>(Tel: 081 573 7992) | Soap and detergent manufacture |
| **Small businesses** | To be established | Owner-managers, employees in small business start ups; business counselling |
| **Small tool/ plant hire** | Mr M Hanrahan<br>Hire Association of Europe<br>722 College Road<br>Erdington<br>Birmingham<br>B44 0AJ<br>(Tel: 021 382 1743) | Small tool/plant hire |
| **Sound** | Mr P Turner<br>Training Initiative for<br>   Professional Sound<br>Sandwell College<br>Woden Road South<br>Wednesbury Sandwell<br>West Midlands<br>WS10 0PE<br>(Tel: 021 556 6000) | |
| **Sport & Recreation** | Mrs J Stock<br>Local Government Training<br>   Board<br>Arndale House<br>The Arndale Centre<br>Luton<br>LU1 2TS<br>(Tel: 0582 451166) | All aspects of leisure and recreation |

| Sector | Lead body | Coverage |
| --- | --- | --- |
| Steel | Mr C D A Green<br>British Steel Corp<br>Ashborne Hill College<br>Ashborne Hll<br>Leamington Spa<br>Warwickshire<br>CV33 9QW<br>(Tel: 0926 651 321) | Natural iron and<br>steel production |
| | Ms L Millington<br>Steel Training Limited<br>NISTA<br>Staybright Works<br>Weedon Street<br>Sheffield<br>S9 2FU<br>(Tel: 0742 446833)<br>(Both part of a consortium for<br>the steel industry) | Steel manufacture<br>and stockholders |
| Sugar | Mr A Brookfield<br>UK Sugar Industry Association<br>British Sugar Plc<br>PO Box 26<br>Oundle Road<br>Peterborough<br>PE2 92U<br>(Tel: 0733 63171) | Manufacture and<br>distribution of<br>sugar and sugar<br>by-products |
| Tele-<br>communications | Mr S McGovern<br>Industrial Relations Adviser<br>Group Personnel GP3<br>Room A460<br>BT Centre<br>81 Newgate Street<br>London<br>EC1A 7AJ<br>(Tel: 071 356 4760) | Telecommunications |

| Sector | Lead body | Coverage |
| --- | --- | --- |
| **Textile manufacture** | National Textile Training Group c/o J Young KLITRA 7 Gregory Boulevard Nottingham NG7 GLD (Tel: 0602 623311) | Manufacture of wool, cotton and related fibres, household textiles, man-made-fibre carpets, narrow fabrics, knitting and lace |
| **Thatching** | Mr G W Nunn Chairman Thatching Standards Committee Rural Development Commission 141 Castle Street Salisbury Wilts SP1 3TP (Tel: 0722 336255 Fax: 0722 332769) | Thatching craft small business competences |
| **Theatre technicians** | Mr G Walne Arts and Entertainments Technical Training Initiative 219 Bunyan Court Barbican London EC2Y 8DH | |
| **Timber** | Mr J Hickmott Timber Trades Federation Clareville House 26 Oxendon Street London SW1Y 4EL (Tel: 071 839 1891) (Part of the Furniture and timber sector) | Timber import and sales |

| Sector | Lead body | Coverage |
| --- | --- | --- |
| **Tobacco** | Mr J A Liddle<br>Chairman<br>Tobacco Industry Training<br>   Organisation<br>Glen House<br>Stag Place<br>London<br>SW1E 5AG<br>(Tel: 071 828 2803) | Processing,<br>distribution of<br>tobacco/tobacco<br>products |
| **Tourism and leisure** | Leisure & Tourism<br>c/o Rob Gent<br>W449 Training Agency<br>Moorfoot<br>Sheffield<br>S1 4PQ | All areas of<br>standards<br>development within<br>tourism; common<br>skills and dormant<br>sector development<br>within the tourism<br>training initiative |
| **Training and Development** | Mr A Graham<br>Chairman<br>TDLB Policy Group<br>The Industrial Society<br>1–23 Southampton Row<br>London<br>WC1B 5HA<br>(Tel: 071 831 8388)<br><br>Mr R A Shepherd<br>Chairman<br>TDLB Employment Advisory<br>   Group<br>41 Hall Lane<br>Upminster<br>Essex<br>RM14 1MF<br>(Tel: 04022 24696) | All those engaged in<br>training or<br>developing others<br>at organisational<br>or individual level |

| Sector | Lead body | Coverage |
| --- | --- | --- |
| | Dr G Tolley<br>Chairman<br>TDLB Professional Advisory<br>  Group<br>74 Furniss Avenue<br>Dore<br>Sheffield<br>S17 3QP<br>(Tel: 0742 360538) | |
| **Wall covering** | Mr M K Levete<br>Wallcovering Manufacturers<br>  Association of Great Britain<br>Alembic House<br>93 Albert Embankment<br>London<br>SE1 7TY<br>(Tel: 071 521 1185) | Wallpaper<br>manufacture |
| **Wastes management** | Mr R A Bispham<br>Secretary<br>WAMITAB<br>3 Albion Place<br>Northampton<br>NN1 1UD | |
| **Water** | Mr P Hall<br>Water Authorities Association<br>1 Queen Anne's Gate<br>London<br>SW1H 9BT<br>(Tel: 071 222 8111) | Water supply and<br>sewage |
| **Wholesale** | Mr V Bingham<br>Chairman<br>National Wholesale Training<br>  Council<br>Regency Court Business Centre<br>62–66 Deansgate | All aspects of<br>wholesaling/<br>warehousing |

| Sector | Lead body | Coverage |
| --- | --- | --- |
| | Manchester M3 2EN (Tel: 061 832 0159) | |
| **Wire and Wire Rope** | Mr G Capper Wire and Wire Rope Employers Association Alpha House Rowlands Way Wythenshaw Manchester M22 5RG (Tel: 061 436 3200) (Now part of the consortium for steel industry) | Manufacture of wire and wire rope |
| **Wool** | R D Clarke Confederation of British Wool Textiles 60 Toller Lane Bradford BD8 9BZ (Tel: 0274 491241) | Manufacture of wool |
| | Mr W Ritchie Scottish Woollen Industry 45 Moray Place Edinburgh EH3 6 EQ (Tel: 031 225 3149) (Both part of NTTG) | |

# Awarding Bodies -List of Abbreviations

**AAT**
The Association of Accounting Technicians

**ABPI**
Association of British Pharmaceutical Industries

**ABRS**
Association of British Riding Schools

**ABTA**
Association of British Travel Agents National Training Board

**BATJIC**
Building and Allied Trades Joint Industrial Council

**BCCCA**
The Biscuit, Cake, Chocolate and Confectionary Alliance

**BCT**
Bus and Coach Training Limited

**BHS**
British Horse Society

**BTEC**
Business and Technician Education Council

**CAPITB**
Clothing & Allied Products Industries Training Board

**CCBC**
The China Clay & Ball Clay Industries Training Board

**CFA**
Contract Flooring Association

**CG**
The City and Guilds of London Institute

**CIA**
Chemical Industries Association

**CITB**
Construction Industry Training Board

**CITB (NI)**
Construction Industry Training Board (Northern Ireland)

**COSIT**
The Computing Services
Industry Training Council

**EITB**
Engineering Industry Training
Board

**EITB(NI)**
Engineering Industry Training
Board (Northern Ireland)

**ETA**
Electricity Training Association

**GTL**
Glass Training Limited

**HCTC**
Hotel and Catering Training
Company

**HTB**
Hairdressing Training Board

**HVDE**
Heating, Ventilating &
Domestic Engineers Nat. Joint
Indust. Council

**IMEAT**
Institute of Meat

**JCBCENI**
Joint Council for the Building
& Civil Engineering Industry of
Northern Ireland

**JCHHT**
The Joint Committee for Heavy
Horse Training

**JIBECI**
Joint Industry Board for the
Electrical Contracting Industry

**LCCI**
The London Chamber of
Commerce and Industry
Examinations Board

**MMFITAB**
Man-made Fibres Industry
Training Advisory Board

**MOD**
Ministry of Defence (Army
Department)

**MTA**
Marine Training Association

**NEBAH**
National Examinations Board
for Argiculture, Horticulture &
Allied Industries

**NFRC**
National Federation of Roofing
Contractors

**NJCBI**
National Joint Council for the
Building Industry

**NJCFGI**
National Joint Council for the
Flat Glass Industry

**NJCFRCI**
National Joint Council for the
Felt Roofing Contracting
Industry

**NJCMAI**
National Joint Council for
Laying side of the Mastic
Asphalt Industry

**NJCMVRRI**
National Joint Council for the Motor Vehicle Retail & Repair Industry

**NJTC**
National Jnt Training Committee for Young Heavy Good Vehicle Drivers

**NPS**
National Pony Society

**NPTC**
National Proficiency Test Council

**NRTC**
National Retail Training Council

**PEI**
Pitman Examinations Institute

**PMI**
Pensions Management Institute

**PPITB**
Plastics Processing Industry Training Board

**PTF**
Petroleum Training Federation

**PTRSW**
Pony Trekking & Riding Society of Wales

**RCP**
Refractories, Clay Pipes & Allied Industries Training Council

**RSA**
RSA Examinations Board

**RTITB**
Road Transport Industry Training Board

**RTITB(NI)**
Road Transport Industry Training Board (Northern Ireland)

**SILB**
Steel Industry Lead Body

**TITO**
Tobacco Industry Training Organisation

# Glossary of Terms

**Accreditation** Formal recognition that individuals have shown evidence of performance which meets specified standards.

**Assessment (competence-based)** Collection of evidence of performance by a variety of methods.

**Awards** A general term for qualifications issued by examining or validating bodies, ie certificates, diplomas etc.

**Awarding body** An examining or validating body. In a competence-based system, an awarding body has central responsibility for the quality, but not the methods of assessment.

**Competence** The ability to perform a particular activity to a prescribed standard. Competence is a wide concept which embodies the ability to transfer skills and knowledge to new situations within the occupational area. It encompasses organisation and planning of work, innovation and coping with non-routine activities. It includes those qualities of personal effectiveness that are required in the workplace to deal with co-workers, managers and customers.

**Continuous assessment** Assessment of competence on every occasion it is required during normal workplace activity. Used for formative assessment and to arrive at a cumulative judgement for final assessment purposes.

**Credit accumulation**   A system by which individuals can accumulate units of competence. When a specified combination of units has been achieved the individual can obtain a full NVQ.

**Credit transfer**   The use of an award (or credits towards one) as credit towards another award.

**Element of competence**   The descriptors of the activities necessary for the completion of the function described in a unit of competence.

**Formative assessment**   Assessment during a course, or over a period of workplace activity which collects evidence of performance.

**Industry Lead Body**   An organisation comprised of industry education and trades union representatives with formal responsibility for the  development of national standards of occupational competence and a framework of National Vocational Qualifications.

**Moderation**   A process or procedure to align standards of assessment between different test papers, different testing occasions, different examiners, different centres etc.

**National Vocational Qualification**   A statement of competence defined by industry and based on nationally agreed standards of occupational competence.

**Norm-referenced assessment**   Assessment of an individual's ability in order to determine how well it compares with other individuals' abilities.

**Performance criteria**   Descriptors of required outcomes of workplace activities.

**Range statements**  Descriptors of the limits within which performance to the identified standard is expected if an individual is to be deemed competent. Range describes competent workplace performance, not the situations in which performance must be observed for assessment purposes.

**Unit of competence**  A descriptor of a discrete function carried out by an individual within an occupational area.

**Underpinning skills and knowledge**  Identifies the knowledge and skill necessary to perform to the standards identified by the performance criteria in the contexts identified in the range statement.

# Who to Contact

| | |
|---|---|
| What NVQs are available? | Regular NCVQ update booklet, *Progress to Date*, from NCV Qualifications 222 Euston Road London NW1 2BZ |
| What standards are available? | Relevant Industry Lead body (ILB) (see list on p 199–237) |
| What standards are under development (if no ILB)? | Training Enterprise and Education Directorate (TEED) Qualifications and Standards Branch Room E454 Moorfoot Sheffield S1 4PQ |
| | *Standards Digest* available from TEED (above) |
| | Relevant awarding body |
| | City and Guilds 46 Britannia Street London WC1X 9RG |
| | BTEC Central House Woburn Place London WC1H 0HH |

RSA
Westwood Way
Coventry
CV4 8HS

| | |
|---|---|
| How do you get access to the NCVQ database? | NCVQ<br>222 Euston Road<br>London<br>NW1 2BZ |
| What NVQs are available? | NCVQ database (above) or relevant Industry Lead Body |
| How do you get in-company training recognised for credit exemption/advanced standing? | your local college/poly or CNAA<br>Grays Inn Road<br>London<br>WC1X 8BP |
| What about qualifications in Scotland (SVQs)? | Scotvec<br>Hanover House<br>Douglas St<br>Glasgow<br>G2 7NQ |

NB NCVQ will be publishing a new briefing series on February 8th 1991. These can be obtained direct from NCVQ publications dept.

# References

BTEC (1990) *APL: General Guidelines* Business and Technician Education Council: London.

CGLI (1988) *Assessment and Validation Procedures for APL* City and Guilds: London.

C&G (1990)*Guidelines on Accreditation of Prior Learning* City and Guilds: London.

CNAA (1984) *Access to Higher Education. Non-standards entry to CNAA first degree and Dip HE courses* Council for National Academic Awards: London.

Coopers and Lybrand (1985) *A Challenge to Complacency Changing Attitudes to Training* Manpower Services Commission/National Economic Development Commission: Sheffield.

Employment Dept (1991) *Development of Assessable Standards for National Certification* Standards/Methodology Unit (edited by Edward Fennell) HMSO: London

NEDC/MSC (1984) *Competence and Competition: Training and Education in the Federal Republic of Germany, The United States and Japan* National Economic Development Office and Manpower Services Commission: Sheffield.

HMSO (1986) *Working Together, Education and Training* Government White Paper Cmnd 9823, Department of Employment, HMSO: London.

MSC (1981) *A New Training Initiative: Agenda for Action* Manpower Services Commission: Sheffield.

MSC/NEDC (1986) Review of Vocational Qualifications in England and Wales

NCVQ (1988a) *The NVQ Criteria and Related Guidance* NCVQ: London.

NCVQ (1988b) *NVQs – What They Mean for You – A Guide*

NCVQ (1988c) *Draft Corporate Plan 1988/9 – 1991/2* NCVQ: London.

NCVQ (1989) 'Occupational standards for dental surgery assistants', *NCVQ R&D Report*, 1, December

NCVQ (quarterly) *Progress to Date*, NCVQ: London.

Randell, G. *Staff Appraisal* Institute of Personnel Management: London.

Scotvec (1988) *The National Certificate. A Guide to Assessment* Scotvec: Glasgow.

Training Agency (1988/90) Competence and Assessment. Standards Methodology Unit, Moorfoot, Sheffield.

# Index